PRAISE FOR *BREAKING UP WITH BABEL*

There is NOBODY like Nikki when it comes to teaching on all things sexuality. Our society is obsessed with this topic and TikTok is shaping this generation's worldview. Is it no wonder they have become the most unhappy one in history? The truth Nikki brings into this space is life changing. Her message is honest yet filled with compassion for the many who have been left broken. There is good news when it comes to our sexuality and it is found in the Bible! Nikki is the biology theology expert, and I have personally watched how people lean in and can't get enough of her teaching. We are so excited she has made her message accessible to everyone through this book because this generation desperately needs to hear it.

—**Cam and Renee Bennett,**
National Youth Alive Directors, Australia

As a former senior pastor, and current leader of the many ACC churches in NSW/ACT, I am constantly looking for ways to empower Christians to engage with and disciple the next generation. Whether we like it or not, sexuality and relationships are part of this conversation, and the sexual message in Scripture is only becoming more significant as we connect with the generation outside the walls of our Sunday services. In her new book Breaking Up with Babel, Nikki unapologetically takes on the subject of sex, dating and relationships in a way that not only gives Christians confidence in their Bibles but a message of hope and restoration for unbelievers! Nikki offers profound tools for those who want to challenge culture and champion purity, as well as holy hope for the questioning, confused and broken. I cannot recommend this book enough to those who are passionate about reaching their generation in a tangible and powerful way.

—**Paul Bartlett, ACC (Australian Christian Churches) NSW & ACT**
State President & ACC National Director for Community Engagement

As a senior pastor with a large percentage of youth and young adults, I am conscious of equipping the next generation with biblical truths around sexuality and identity. Nikki's book is a word in season for pastors, youth pastors and leaders, scripture teachers, parents, young adults and youth. Nikki is brilliant and gifted at explaining deep and complex truths in a way that is retainable and relatable to the young modern reader. When it comes to living out Christian values, this book will give you the often unexplained 'why's' behind 'what' we believe in relation to identity and sexuality. I believe this book is going to become a pivotal tool for training the next generation. I highly recommend this book from both a pastoral perspective, and as a mother of three pre-teen children. I am grateful to have it as a resource in my life and ministry.

—**Louise Antonius, Senior Pastor Eastcoast Church, Australian Christian Churches NSW & ACT Executive**

We are living in extraordinary times! Biblical language and its clear definitions of human sexuality and sexual wholeness are being aggressively challenged. For example, there is an accelerating agenda to "break the binary." This is the latest expression of the language of Babel. While this book reestablishes a biblical model of dating and sexual wholeness, Nikki Dent's revolutionary book courageously "celebrates the binary" and gives much-needed guidance in delivering us from the confusing language of Babel. I will be recommending this book to everyone!

—**Phil Mason, Senior Pastor Tribe Church, Founder of the Heart Revolution Network**

What a timely publication! *Breaking Up with Babel* is a brilliant, well-written book and holds the keys to success regarding the much-misunderstood topic of sex, dating and relationships. Nikki has spent many years in our town of Byron Bay (the perfect backdrop to this book) and has seen first-hand that the world's values in this area create nothing short of a mess in every sphere of life! We were created for holiness, which, in short, means "set apart to God". It's not a popular idea, but it is the master key to our freedom! A high-end biblical worldview is the medicine we need in a world of confusion and fear. This book holds the key to healing and wholeness for all seeking understanding around relationships. Thank you, Nikki, for being bold and clear!

—**Maria Mason, Senior Pastor Tribe Church,**
Founder of the Heart Revolution Network

BREAKING UP WITH BABEL

THE GOSPEL OF SEX,
DATING, AND RELATING
IN A CULTURE OF
CONFUSION

BREAKING UP WITH BABEL

NIKKI DENT

© 2023 Nikki Dent

All rights reserved. No part of this publication may be reproduced, stored in a retrieval system, or transmitted in any form or by any means – for example, electronic, photocopy, recording – without the prior written permission of the publisher. The only exception is brief quotations in printed reviews.

Published by Breaking Up With Babel
www.breakingupwithbabel.com
Instagram: @breakingupwithbabel

Printed in Australia

Unless otherwise indicated, all Scripture quotations are taken from the Holy Bible, New Living Translation, copyright © 1996, 2004, 2015 by Tyndale House Foundation. Used by permission of Tyndale House Publishers, Carol Stream, Illinois 60188. All rights reserved.

Scripture quotations marked (NIV) are taken from the Holy Bible, New International Version®, NIV®. Copyright © 1973, 1978, 1984, 2011 by Biblica, Inc.™ Used by permission of Zondervan. All rights reserved worldwide. www.zondervan.com The "NIV" and "New International Version" are trademarks registered in the United States Patent and Trademark Office by Biblica, Inc.™

Scripture quotations taken from the (NASB) New American Standard Bible®, Copyright © 1960, 1971, 1977, 1995, 2020 by The Lockman Foundation. Used by permission. All rights reserved. lockman.org

Scripture quotations marked (MSG) are taken from The Message, copyright © 1993, 2002, 2018 by Eugene H. Peterson. Used by permission of NavPress. All rights reserved. Represented by Tyndale House Publishers.

Scripture quotations marked (BSB) are taken from The Holy Bible, Berean Standard Bible, BSB. Copyright ©2016, 2020 by Bible Hub. Used by Permission. All Rights Reserved Worldwide.

Scripture quotations marked (KJV) are taken from the King James Version of the Holy Bible.

Editing by Virginia Bashkar
Book design & typesetting by Typography Studio

ISBN: 978-0-6457229-0-1

Mum and Dad: You have quietly and humbly preached the Gospel to us by your consistent affection and devotion to one another. Because of you, I am. Congratulations on 40 years.

Paul: For showing me that men can be sons of God, outstanding fathers, and exceptional husbands. You are simply above and beyond, proving to me daily that God's way is the way to rich and joyful blessing. You are the evidence. And our daughters are most blessed to witness it.

Lou: For coming on the garden journey with me, from when this book was just a seed, all the way to fruition. You have fertilised this project with much prophetic encouragement and prayer, and I am quite sure this book would not have happened if not for your constant stream of supportive coaxing. Thankyou for valuing these words and loving the next generation enough to tell them the truth.

Pastor Sue and Neville: For leading me up the garden path first. You have handed me a bag of seeds full of your own knowledge and teachings, and graciously allowed me to sow them into other fields as if they were my own. This book would not only be full of holes and lacking much colour and depth without Neville's decades of insight and creative brilliance in his presentation of the gospel and covenant, but it probably would not exist.

Contents

Introduction	xiii
1. Gardens and Towers	1
2. The Sexual Gospel	23
3. Biology Theology	43
4. When Two Become One	59
5. Men and Women in the Image of God	79
6. Boundaries to Blessings	103
7. Dating in a Digital World	125
8. The Gift of Singleness	151
9. Babel's Table	167
10. Breaking Up with Babel	187
Endnotes	207

Introduction

I f you ever find yourself on an island with no fresh drinking water, knowing how to purify and desalinate salt water can mean the difference between life and death. Behold *distillation*. I know most of you reading have graduated beyond high school science class and have no intention of taking another lesson! Even if you have no plans to get stranded anytime soon, allow me to explain this crucial process. To distil a liquid is to purify it by heating and cooling. The heat causes it to vaporise, and then after the vapours cool and condense, the resulting purified and precious liquid may be collected as clean water. Simply, distillation removes the volatile content – in this case, salt – from a mixture by heating. In fact, to remove the volatile components, the liquid must first reach a *rollicking* boiling point.

I don't know about you, but when I switch on the TV, scan my social media feed, or observe pop culture, it seems

INTRODUCTION

modern society has reached a boiling point when it comes to relationships. "Volatile" is an apt description of the nature of our conversations, especially where the Christian worldview conflicts with cultural trends. Things have gotten pretty salty. When it comes to relationships, we've reached a rollicking collision of two worldviews: Christianity and secular humanism.

Humanism is what we're left with when humanity abandons God as the source and measure of what is true, moral, ethical, and beautiful, and we are left to define these things ourselves. If we don't have our God and our Bible, we have no choice but to make *ourselves* god, and create our *own* morality. This is not a new phenomenon, but rather the product of a conflict as old as Genesis. The first book of your Bible records humanity's rebellion against their benevolent Creator as a result of swallowing a poisonous seed of deception. In this book, we're going to explore how Scripture's record of the first humans in the Garden of Eden provides us with an unfailing vision for cultivating fruitful relationships, marriage, and sex. However, over and against this "Garden" vision, the ugly Tower of Babel emerges but a few chapters later. Instead of garden-growing, Babel offers a tower-building culture as a humanistic alternative. An alternative that says, "I want to do this my way, outside of God's will and command."

In this book, let's observe the parallels between modern humanistic culture and Babel culture. After all, they share a common ancestor: one that has been hissing lies to us from the soil of Eden. For illustrative purposes, I'll refer to modern

INTRODUCTION

secular culture as "Hollywood culture" or "Hollywood." This is not a criticism of the district of Los Angeles, the art of film making, or film watching. Rather, it's a euphemism for the feelings-based, hormones-driven, sexually immoral worldview that is perpetuated in popular films, media, and the lifestyles of many celebrities that dominate reality TV and much of our social media. In essence, *"Hollywood"* is no longer simply a film-making industry. It is a culture in and of itself, permeating screens, magazines, and endlessly scrolled feeds – it is Babel dressed up in modern glitz and glamour. In this way, contemporary culture is simply the product of a society that has drifted from its biblical roots. Once upon a time, the western world was founded upon biblical revelation. The laws, the education, the society. These roots once resulted in the flowering of truth, where right and wrong, identity, intelligent origins, and eternal destiny were clearly defined. As people reject the authority of Scripture, it should not surprise us that people are beginning to think of truth as *fluid*. "Your truth" may now be different to "my truth" which sounds benevolent but has disastrous consequences. You see, for truth to be truth, it cannot be subjective. It can't be influenced by opinions, feelings, or influencers in the wild. When you enter a court of law, it becomes very important to discover what the truth is. Suddenly truth *must* be absolute and unchanging to make sense and inspire conviction and compassion. The trending concept of subjective truth falls in on itself. Ultimately, if truth is fluid, you cannot prove anything, the laws

INTRODUCTION

of society fall over, life has no meaning, morality cannot be defined, and neither our origins nor our destiny can be certain. Behold, the end game of *modern humanism* – the apex of Babel.

In a society that is moving away from absolutes, it's a natural by-product that people are confused. They're sexually confused. They're morally confused. They're confused about identity. They're unsure of where they came from and where they'll end up. Rather than think about these things too deeply, Babel culture provides various manifestos to mask the problem, whether it's the current *"Live Your Truth"*, or the old millennial *"YOLO!"* (You Only Live Once) or even as the ancient Corinthians chanted *"eat, drink, for tomorrow we die"* (1 Cor 15:32). Translation: Live life without much regard to consequences, restraint, or limits. Squeeze as much self-pleasure out of every moment you can because there isn't much point to life outside of that.

When we abandon truth, chaos and confusion ensue. From the media to the classroom, the beliefs of Christianity are being questioned, challenged, and even oppressed regarding sex, dating, and relating. In this book, as we contrast Hollywood's ideals to the Bible's sexual worldview, we will thrust our confusion into the light of Scripture. Chaos and confusion can give way to order, design, and life. Rotten fruit can be forfeited for something wholesome, healthy, fruitful, and joyful. I'm personally pretty optimistic about the future – as God's people challenge culture and champion truth, I believe

INTRODUCTION

many of the confused and broken will turn to the hope of the gospel and be saved.

Holding a radical position regarding sexuality is not something exclusive to our generation, of course. Roll the tape back to ancient Rome, where pornography was etched into the walls of homes, men were physically castrating themselves in pagan worship, and a sexually chaotic culture paid tribute to a long list of gods and goddesses that supposedly controlled daily life. Into *this* culture the early Church inaugurated a sexual revolution – one that fled sexual immorality and restored sex to its rightful and dignified place: inside the confines of monogamous marriage, used for the express purpose of blessing one another in a symphony of trust and honour. Hellenistic hedonism collided with the worldview of monotheistic Christianity. Yes, the gospel permeated the sex lives of the early Christians as much as it does today.

But the tape doesn't stop there. We must go back further. As they laid the first brick of the Tower of Babel, two worlds were at odds with one another: God's idea and the human idea. It is here we see that the world has always attempted to suffocate God's seeds with bricks, and modern culture is no exception. God has always commanded us to cultivate gardens, and we have always tried to build towers. He has always asked us to submit to Him and grow healthy and beautiful things. We have always tried to take short cuts and build our own way.

Is this a reason to fret, giving into secular arguments, or giving up on being faithful? If Church history and Scripture itself

INTRODUCTION

has anything to say on the matter, the answer is a resounding "No!" When an idea is challenged, we intuitively make a greater effort to define it. We consider it from every angle to justly defend and stand by it. A process of distillation takes place where the heat of adversity eradicates impure components and extracts the precious and true meaning. For this reason, the word "distil" is used in the English language to describe the extraction of essential meaning or the most important aspects of something. Friends, we are undergoing a much-needed *distillery process* in the domain of relationships! The heat of criticism and debate is squeezing truth out of us – the meaning of sex, dating, and relationships is only becoming richer and more beautiful for those determined to forsake Hollywood and hold fast to the Holy Wood of Christ.

If you don't believe me, just take a look at your Bible. The very reason you have a closed canon of Scripture is because its truth was opposed. Heresies that challenged the early Church caused believers to think more deeply about what they believe. They wrestled through the sacred writings, debated heatedly, and held councils. Creeds and carefully curated doctrine were painfully birthed in response to false teachings that had reached a rollicking boiling point in those days! The crucible of opposition crystallized into the canon and creeds that we now hold so dear, strengthening and building the Church to this very day. My point is this: The doctrine, ideas, and scriptures we might take for granted were actually hard fought for. And so, paradoxically, what initially might have *threatened* the

INTRODUCTION

Church seems only to have fortified and *purified* the Church. The Church has not simply survived – She has thrived and grown in the face of challenge and persecution. She has shifted shape and methodology, perhaps, but never the ancient truth upon which She stands. This otherworldly resilience isn't going to change just because Zuckerberg invented Facebook, algorithms keep us guessing, and people preach loudly against the Christian faith from their digital pulpits.

In the same way, it is no insignificant matter that relationships and sexuality are under fire in our current generation. I truly believe that the Lord Jesus is performing a distillery work in *us*, His Church. No, we are not coming up with any new ideas when it comes to sexuality. But rather we are being forced to extract the ancient and otherworldly truth by eradicating unhelpful and impure information and ideas. Not only that, we are being given an opportunity to present the gospel of restoration and redemption in a unique way as we cherish not "our truth" but *the* Truth.

The challenges and questions to the Christian worldview about romantic relationships are at times both hostile *and* valid. Some are hostile simply because they reject God. Jesus predicted that the world would hate us because they hated Him first (Jn15:18). Some arguments are valid. A biblically illiterate society simply has meaningful questions about Christian sexual values that we should be equipped and willing to answer. As challenges to our faith intensify in the news, media platforms, and high school corridors, some believers react in

INTRODUCTION

aggressive defence, using our Bibles (and keyboards) to beat a secular society into submission to our beliefs. At the other end of the spectrum, Christians have recoiled in compromise, succumbing to a Christian-Babel hybrid, where Biblical ideals are stretched to accommodate an increasingly depraved sexual ethic. However, we needn't swing to either extreme. Challenges to our worldview should cause us to think more deeply about what it is we believe and *why*. Why should we wait until marriage to have sex? Why should we marry someone who is also a believer? Why is porn and masturbation not only a sin, but a really terrible idea for any human who wants to be sexually healthy? Speaking of, what defines health anyway? It is my hope that this book contributes to helping us think deeply about our ancient-yet-timeless worldview when it comes to sex and relationships. Another drop in the glass of fresh water being distilled through the bubbling and boiling conversations of our generation!

The profound hope we have is that the jostling and loud voices that appear to threaten the Church could be the very thing that purifies Her. We will emerge *more* convinced of this truth of old as it reaches into every area of our lives, relationships, and sexuality. Rather than imitating those who traverse the road to Babel, maybe we'll birth an entirely redeemed culture through the timeless Word of God. Perhaps the relational crisis in our generation will produce more and more books such as this, that together form a bedrock of certainty for those who tread the narrow Garden path. We will wrestle through

INTRODUCTION

the questions and fight for a foundation that those who come after us – our children and grandchildren – can stand upon with bold and joyful conviction.

Remember, distilling requires volatile heating followed by cooling. Yes, the heated debates around sex, dating, and relating in our culture can feel a little too hot to handle at times. But rest assured that when we bring these conversations and conflicts into the cooling presence of Christ and His Word, we will extract the pure vision for our relationships. A vision in which commands are transfigured into promises. A vision so precious we will treasure it for all our days, as we would a gold wedding band, a diamond engagement ring, or a set of wedding vows.

I invite you, my friend, to come on a distilling journey with me. Let's think more deeply about what we believe, remembering the profound prophecy of Ezekiel as he foresaw distilling waters of the Holy Spirit: *"The waters of this stream will make the salty waters of the Dead Sea fresh and pure"* (Ezekiel 47:8).

Gardens and Towers

This book is about *relationships*, but before we launch into sex, dating, and relating (as a former youth pastor I know some might be tempted to skip ahead to those chapters!), let us consider the cruciality of healthy relationships. While the backdrop of the Bible is a *collectivist* society, where the community is prioritised, our modern western culture is an *individualistic* society, where the individual is prioritised. This is important, because this increase in individualistic thinking has dulled our relational senses. Promoting the idea of being self-reliant and independent has in some ways benumbed us to our acute need and value for community. Western individualism therefore tempts us to think our relationships are a private affair; that relationships, marriages, sexuality, and families have nothing to do with anyone else, so they can mind their own business! Friends, it's so much grander than that. Healthy relationships are to be the vehicle that

God is using to build His Kingdom upon this earth. Does that sound like an exaggeration? We're going to dive into Genesis and discover why it's not.

As I mentioned before, the current relational epidemic we'll explore in this book is not a modern ailment. It had a genesis, finding its origin in the opening pages of humanity's collective story. The first book of your Bible records the aetiology of soiled relationships.[1] This is fortunate, because if you're in the medical field, you'll know that discovering the root cause is always the route to the remedy. Pain is a signal that points to the deeper problem. Naturally, Scripture reveals both the disease and the antidote. It's time we quit masking symptoms in our aching generation and pursue healed and whole relationships. Come friend, let's dispose of our social Band-Aids and pull out our Bibles.

The Original Relationship

Genesis 1:1 "In the beginning God..."

It shouldn't surprise us that when we open the Word of God we're immediately introduced to a relationship. Right at the beginning, before time ticked its first tock, there was the Trinity. The Father, the Son (the Creator-Word) and the Spirit hovering; all working in a perfect relationship of harmonious equality to bestow life, blessing, and fruitfulness to what many of our Bible translations call "emptiness" and "darkness." If we're going to explore healthy relationships (including healthy dating and healthy sexuality) we need to go back to the source of it all: God. He *is* relationship. He is what we call a perichoretic community, mutually indwelling in perfect unity. The stunning mystery we call "the Godhead."

The Trinity may baffle us, but in a strange way it makes sense, perfectly explaining humankind's desperate need for wholesome relationships. Even the scientists and spirituals agree on this one: Wholesome relationship is built into our D.N.A, and this desperate need in the soul of every human is simply a reflection of our Maker. God is in relationship, and if we are made in that image, it makes sense that we need relationship to be truly human.[2] And not just any relationships – we need *good* relationships. Flourishing, healthy, honest, and intimate relationships. The kind of relationships grounded in the soil of real *life*, not *likes*. Relationships that give space for real *emotions*, not *emojis*. Relationship with real *people*, not *profiles*.

Imago Dei

Genesis 1:26–27 reads: "Then God said, "Let us make human beings in *our* image, to be like *us*. They will reign over the fish in the sea, the birds in the sky, the livestock, all the wild animals on the earth, and the small animals that scurry along the ground." So God created human beings in his own image. In the image of God he created them; male and female he created them" (emphasis mine). Notice that God says let "us" (the Trinity) make humankind in "our" image. In other words, we bear the image of the One who is Perfect Relationship. Therefore, when God first makes humanity, He doesn't make one person, but two. Eve isn't created from the dust, as Adam is. Eve is pulled from the very flesh and bone of Adam, because from one flesh God made two humans. As much as some of us love staying at home with our cats, we cannot wholly image Him in isolation – we image God as we relate to one another in a special oneness. In fact, Genesis 2:18 tells us that the only thing in God's creation that is decidedly not good is Adam lacking this vital aspect of what makes him human: horizontal relationship. And yes, it's supposed to stick out in the narrative like a sore thumb. So, guess what we've just discovered on the first page of our Bible? We're created to bear the image of God – and it can't be done without holy relationships! When COVID restrictions separated us from each other, we were plunged into a world of temporary but involuntary isolation. The spike in mental illness during these periods of isolation only exposed this innate truth, even for the most introverted person.

The point is this: Relationship is not only God's *idea,* it's who He *is.* If we're made in His image, we, too, are created for harmonious and powerful relationships. When we get it right, we image Him clearer than ever, and so fulfil our calling. Christians should, of course, be the most equipped people at cultivating relationships because we personally know the manufacturer. And just like the OG relationship "in the beginning," our relationships are supposed to bear fruit and bestow blessing to a world consumed in emptiness and darkness. How so? What evidence do we have that our relationships are really that powerful and important? Keep reading.

The Garden

If we glance at the verse that comes directly and inseparably after Genesis 1:27, we'll see that after God tells us who we *are* (male and female image-bearers) He tells us what to *do:* "Then God blessed them and said "Be *fruitful* and *multiply*. Fill the earth and *govern* it. *Reign* over the fish in the sea, the birds in the sky, and all the animals that scurry along the ground" (Gen 1:28, emphasis mine).

There is always a mission attached to the message. God creates us in His image, but now He outlines what imaging him is actually going to look like in practice. Governing and reigning is the vocabulary of *power*. Being fruitful and multiplying is the vocabulary of *relationship*. So embedded in His decision to make us image-bearers is the challenge to use this *power* given to us to build *relationships,* and therefore build His Kingdom upon His earth. I'm not sure if you've considered this, but being made in the image of God makes us very powerful creatures. Genesis reveals that we're given more authority than the animals, the plants, and anything else on the planet. Newsflash: we're meant to use this power to *be fruitful and multiply*. To be powerful, holy, Kingdom people who produce *more* powerful, holy, Kingdom people. As relationships flourish, communities, societies, and governments will flourish. On the flip-side, this power can be as much a curse as it is a blessing – if relationships break down, these very same constituents will slowly decompose.

Take note where all of this takes place: in a garden! God even uses agricultural language to describe the calling of every image-bearer: *Be fruitful and multiply! Spread out across the whole earth* – in other words, grow! Grow my Kingdom, kids. Grow it in the context of wholesome relationships, using the power I've bestowed upon you, not *against* each other but *with* one another. Under Me, and over Creation.[3]

This is what many theologians call the "incomplete completion" of the creation account.[4] God deliberately left Creation opulent and ideal, but "incomplete" in the sense that the goal was always for humanity to *continue* building the garden. In other words, Eden was never supposed to stay Eden. They were supposed to take this garden environment they'd been given and grow it *outward*, across the earth, advancing the Kingdom of God.[5] They'd do it side by side, in the winsome diversity that comes from femaleness and maleness, and a holy unity that comes from being of the same flesh.

I propose that since the beginning of time we were supposed to cultivate relationships like you'd grow a garden – and in doing so, grow His Kingdom. I don't know about you, but

I'm beginning to realise why the Enemy launched such an immediate assault on the male-female relationship. He sniffed out the potential right from the beginning, and when he imagined what could be birthed through this kind of healthy harmony... well, feeling *threatened* is an understatement. And so, before we can really even brainstorm what this staggering enterprise could even look like, Satan slithers into action and tempts Adam and Eve with a certain tree (of the knowledge of good and evil) and uses it to drive a wedge between them.[6]

The First Toxic Relationship

Most of us know how the story goes. The first humans are tempted by Satan with the idea of using this unique relational power *outside* of God's instruction and authority. It's a diabolical strategy from that wretched lizard – subtle, but catastrophic in its ramifications. Genesis 3:4–5 says: "'You won't die!' the serpent replied to the woman. 'God knows that your eyes will be opened as soon as you eat it, and you will be like God, knowing both good and evil.'" Satan was selling the same humanism that is rife in the twenty-first century. Humanism as we know it is just another way of *playing God*, dressed up in prettier language. When we thumb the pages of history, we see that doing things our way instead of God's way has never gone well for us, especially in the realm of relationships, and definitely when it comes to sex. The Fall of humanity that resulted when Eve and Adam succumbed to temptation was not just a stumble – it was a plummet. Both Creation and humanity were cursed, and did you notice the first thing impacted? That's right. *Relationships.*

We're only three chapters into our Bible and we find the relationships between God and humanity (vertical) and between Adam and Eve (horizontal) are now horribly fractured. What should have been side-by-side dominion between the first couple will mutate into *domination.* Fostering community will be substituted for *control.* Serving will uglify into *subjugation.* It may not manifest immediately, but the ravages of the Fall deepen with every generation from this point on in Scripture until Christ graces the pages of the Gospels and turns the world upside down.

Genesis 3 carries a chilling prediction: "… And you will desire to control your husband, but he will rule over you." Instead of governing and reigning *alongside* one another, men and women will now control and rule *over* one another.

Power struggle and conflict punctures the human experience for the first time in their short history. As a result, they felt shame (Gen 3:7), fear (Gen 3:10), and blame (Gen 3:12).

And if you dig up the soil of every relational rupture, every toxic couple, every broken heart and bad break up, you will still discover these ancient-but-poisonous roots of shame, fear, blame and power struggle. It was never meant to be, but this is where rebellion (even when it's cloaked in Hollywood humanism) will lead us.

We were meant to extend the Kingdom of God, like an ever-growing garden twisting and creeping into people's lives and blossoming into fruitful families, marriages, churches, and communities. But alas, instead of building God's Kingdom, we ended up building our own. If you'll skip forward a few more chapters with me, you'll see this play out spectacularly. By the time we land on Genesis 11, humans are indeed using their power to build – but it's not a garden, sprawling *outward* across the earth, as God commissioned them in the beginning. It's a tower that goes *upward* to the sky![7]

Building in the Image of ... Who?

Here in Genesis, the text unapologetically reveals the insidious motivation behind the building of the Tower of Babel: "They began saying to each other, "Let's make bricks and harden them with fire." (In this region bricks were used instead of stone, and tar was used for mortar.) Then they said, "Come, let's build a great city for ourselves with a tower that reaches into the sky. This will make us famous and keep us from being scattered all over the world." (11:3–4)

As we read the text, we observe a grand attempt at building something, but it's kind of the opposite of what God asked. What they're building is a ziggurat, which was a common form of pagan worship in the Mesopotamian culture at the time. They were towers with a temple on top, where one would attempt to barter and manipulate the gods to get power. But if we get down to it, they're simply building in the image of the surrounding culture. Instead of trying to be fruitful, humanity is trying to be famous. And honestly, not that much has changed as we stroke the glass screens of our smartphones! In just nine short verses, we see a spectacle of creatures yet again aspiring to be the Creator – welcome to the Fall: 2.0!

Ok, you ask, but what's this got to do with me? You may never have set foot on a construction site, but everyone is a builder of *some*thing. We're all building, sculpting, measuring, curating; whether it's habits, a marriage, a lifestyle, a church, a business, or a social media presence. So, when it comes to relationships, it's worth asking ourselves: Are we building gardens or Babel? What proverbial "material" are we building with? What's motivating and influencing us? Are we fostering an environment conducive to fruitfulness, health, life, and growth – or are we simply building in the image of the surrounding culture? Because now is as good a time as any to remind you – the surrounding culture might be popular, but that doesn't mean that it's healthy.

Just as our Babel-builders copied the Mesopotamian culture, our generation isn't immune to mimicking the ethos of Hollywood and allowing it to influence the way we approach romance, marriage, family, and sex. We're all tempted at some point to build in the image of social media, cultural trends, and the rich, famous, and successful – rather than in the image of God. I'm not sure if you've noticed, but the lives of the most popular and wealthy don't exactly provide a glowing example of resilient relationships. (In fact, a Hollywood relationship that lasts the test of time is considered an anomaly.)

You and I ought to be diligent as God's people not to return to the ways of Babel. The temptation to copy and image the surrounding culture of the world is as prevalent today as it was in the eleventh chapter of your Bible. Babel was knocked down, but its lure remains, glowing as bright as our phone screens late at night. We're going to find out in this book, that while Babel is big, popular, loud, and influential – it doesn't produce fruit, and it always gets knocked down.

Quicksand Relationships

Why do we get enamoured by Babel-type relationships? Surely we can see through the superficiality of Hollywood romances, where relationships are as cosmetically enhanced as the characters play-acting in them. Deep down we know their lips aren't real, and neither is their love. Yet somehow we can still get hooked into building relationships like they do in your average rom-com, where sexual attraction takes the driver's seat and sacrificial commitment is relegated to the roadside.

I'd like to suggest that it's tempting to build Babel when it comes to relationships because it can be constructed quickly! Now, you might think the idea of making and building a tower is a slow enterprise, but bricks were the latest building technology of Babel times, and they grew much quicker than a seed in the ground! You could say bricks were the smartphone of ancient civilization. They made for much faster building than the alternatives, and we know anything fast is instantly gratifying. You and I can relate. We want satisfying relationships at an accelerated rate, healthy marriages overnight, churches that spring up quickly, businesses that flourish immediately. Quick results lead to quick satisfaction.

We invented microwaves because we want food *now*; internet banking because we want the money in the account *now*; social media platforms to have connection *now*. But it's in the realm of sex and dating that this becomes more complex and even insidious. We invent filters because we want to look good *now*. We download endless dating apps because we want a partner *now*. We turn to pornography because we want sexual gratification *now*.

Today's humans are still attempting to build relationships with bricks – they're just smaller and fit in our back pocket. We're attempting to build love and intimacy through screens, earning us relationships that tower a mile high and an inch deep. As we scroll social media platforms, we unwittingly allow them to sculpt our worldview of what's permissible, beneficial, beautiful, and moral. The surrounding pagan culture compels us to build relationships characterized by image, speed, and quantity. It's *better* to use these proverbial bricks. It's *faster* to make friends on Facebook. It's *easier* to swipe right.

GARDENS AND TOWERS

Did you catch those words? Better, faster, easier – this is the mantra of Babel, and though it has never come good on that promise, it seems to suck us in every time we hear it. It might be impressive as a ziggurat in appearance, but I'm telling you friends, it's a kingdom of digital sand. If Hollywood's statistics tell us anything, these bricks will quickly dissolve into relational *quick*sand. And like this loose, wet sand that yields easily to pressure and sucks in anything resting on or falling into it, Babel relationships can't hold anything substantial.

We know this is the most socially interconnected generation we have ever seen in history, yet somehow it remains unquestionably bereft of true community, true intimacy, and true love. Statistically we're the loneliest and most isolated generation yet to collectively breath on planet Earth (and that was before COVID). We're grappling for a better way to do relationships, but if we're looking to the surrounding culture for inspiration, we're going to sink.

Take a deep inhalation of hope: We might dwell in a Babel generation, but we have a timeless gospel.

In a generation building towers with screens, relationships gauged by height instead of depth, outward appearance instead of inner strength, followers instead of friendship, fame instead of fortitude – I just wonder if we're facing one of the greatest open doors for the gospel we've ever seen. I wonder if God's people will stick out like a green thumb in this landscape of Modern Mesopotamia. Because according to Genesis, God's people don't build the same way that the world builds. We're supposed to build, sculpt, measure and curate our relationships in a way that is radically different to the surrounding culture. We're not building towers, we're growing *gardens*. Sure, seeds might take longer than bricks, but might I remind you they last longer too. Seeds produce fruit that produce more seeds. I don't know if you've noticed, but bricks don't produce more bricks. They just crumble away after a while. Seeds leave a legacy.

The Kingdom way of sex, dating, marriage, and romance might seem slower. It might involve a lot of waiting. It requires self-control and sacrifice. But we're not taking short-cuts or building impressive architecture. We're building something that's meant to last. We're building relationships, marriages and families that leave a *legacy* for future generations.

The Parable of Two Building Approaches

The Gospels of Matthew and Luke record Jesus juxtaposing two kinds of building approaches. We usually identify it as the Parable of the Two Builders. Matthew 7:25–27 says: "Anyone who listens to my teaching and follows it is wise, like a person who builds a house on solid rock. Though the rain comes in torrents and the floodwaters rise and the winds beat against that house, *it won't collapse because it is built on bedrock*. But anyone who hears my teaching and doesn't obey it is foolish, like a person who builds a house on sand. When the rains and floods come and the winds beat against that house, it will *collapse with a mighty crash*" (emphasis mine).

What Jesus, the Word of all Wordsmiths, tells us is that building on rock is a much longer, slower process. The word for "rock" in the Greek here is *petra* (πέτρα) and actually means *bedrock*.[8] You have to dig down to get to the bedrock. It takes time, effort, labour, tools, skills, and fortitude. Relationships built on the bedrock of Christ's Word won't fail. Will they face seasons, storms, difficulties, and conflicts? Of course. Every builder will. *When* life beats against our relationships, our families, our marriages, it'll expose our building strategies. Did we build in accordance with the surrounding culture, or did we build according to the Word of God? Did we use popular trends or biblical principles? And the promise tucked into this parable, spoken by the same Creator that brought life out of what was formless and empty, is that a relationship built on God's Word will stand. It'll endure. It won't be *cancelled*. It won't be swept away in the torrent of Hollywood statistics and divorce rates that yield pain through the generations.

Of course, sand will always be an alluring option. It's seems *better, faster, easier* than bothering to dig down to find the foundation. Building on sand is suitable for the time-poor, the impatient, those looking for quick-fixes, instant gratification, and love in all the wrong places. What you've built might stand for a little while. But will it survive the inevitable shift in seasons? The unpleasant life squalls that can spring up, and even the occasional hurricanes of hell?

Jesus says it'll crash like faulty software.

A Kingdom of Digital Sand

Speaking of software, microchips are said to be the building blocks of technology and the foundations of our digital world. Do you know what microchips are made of? They're printed on silicon wafers, which are made from silica sand. Our entire world of digital technology is quite literally built upon... sand. I'm not saying digital technology, social media, or screens are immoral – and I don't think Jesus is, either. Technology in and of itself is the fruit of the creativity God has instilled in humanity. But anything that enables us to get fast results has grave potential to become immoral. As the familiar adage goes, "With great power comes great responsibility." Digital technology can be beneficial for many things, but a dangerous foundation to build our lives, relationships, and worldview upon. Historians of technology will tell you that technology is always a reflection of the trending values of that society. Even the experts in Silicon Valley will admit that social media is not values-neutral, and never was. Many of the apps that have become the foundation on which many build their social life, are engineered to exploit our psychological vulnerabilities. Even the pull-down refresh mechanism (the one that gives your thumb RSI) is modelled after the slot machines in casinos, devised to keep you using it, and eventually addicted to it. Social media might be a helpful tool for marketing, exchanging information and connecting with people in places we can't physically get to. But friend, it's not the tool you want to build your relationships with.

So, let's put down the phone and pick up a shovel as we consider our final question: what does building in the image of God look like? All this talk of building gardens instead of Babel sounds theoretically great. But how do we build (or, if you like, grow) relationships God's way, instead of the world's way? I intend to spend the rest of this book unpacking this question, but before we go into detail, we must dig down to the bedrock: the gospel.

Imago Christus

You might remember when humanity was exiled from the Garden of Eden, angels prevented their return with flaming swords at the gate (Gen 3:24). Since a sword can threaten death, it eventually became a symbol of controlling power and dominating rule. This is toxic power, a product of the Fall, and it locks us out of the garden.

With this in mind, it is remarkable that Isaiah 2:4 speaks of a day where swords will be hammered into ploughshares. A ploughshare is an agricultural tool. A day will come, he predicts, when the instrument for cursed power will be turned into an instrument for ... gardening? A day will come when the power God gave us in Genesis will be used once again to cultivate beautiful and fruitful things.

I wonder if you've ever imagined how to turn a sword into a ploughshare. Forget the swift results of the pull-down mechanism or instant upload ... it must be slowly beaten, hewn, and hammered over and over until it literally changes shape for a different purpose. Friends, 2000 years ago there was a seed. And that seed eventually grew into a tree. This tree was stripped of its branches, hammered and hewn into an ugly instrument of power, control, and domination. The hands of men had built a wooden Babel, and upon this rugged structure they hung our Saviour. Deuteronomy 21:23 declares "anyone who is hung on a tree is under God's curse." (BSB)

Towering over the disciples who followed Jesus to Golgotha, Babel took its full-fledged form that fateful day of Calvary – the Tree of Death casting its shadow over Roman soldiers and broken Christ-followers alike. What these humans hadn't considered was that before there was ever a garden, a man, a woman, or a serpent – there was *this* cross. There was a perfect plan in motion for redemption before He ever breathed the first soul into Adam (Rev. 13:8, 1 Peter 1:19–20).

Isaiah prophesied of the day that the Tree of Death would be hammered and painfully transformed into a Tree of Life! That wooden sword of ugly Babel power that had *plagued* all of humanity would be transformed into a gardening instrument used to *plough* the hearts of humanity, bringing the healing and transformational power of what you and I call *the gospel*. The curse reversed as the Creator of Seeds hung on our Tree. Harkening back to the very relationships that were broken in the beginning, the cross reaches upwards and outwards – and promises blessing to every Babel-weary heart.

How do we build in the image of God? God's answer to this question is answered in Jesus Christ, when the Creator of the first garden set his feet on earthly soil. Paul's holy boast in Colossians 1:15 proclaims "Christ is the visible image of the invisible God." Jesus Christ is the perfect image-bearer and the truest human. He has unlocked Eden's gates and paved the way back to the Garden. He went to the cross to show us what it truly takes to grow relationships, and therefore grow His Kingdom:

Not technology.
Not bricks and mortar.
Not popular trends.
Not Hollywood.
Not cancel culture.
Not selfies.
Not followers.
Not sliding into DMs.
Not swiping right.

Our relationships must take cruciform. The relationships that last the test of time will be the ones that are driven not by love of self, fame, image, or speed – but by sacrificial, others-oriented, biblical love. Love that is willing to wait. Love that goes slow. Love that endures all seasons, whether enjoyable or excruciating. Love that practices self-control, integrity, and honour. Love that values the person over promiscuity. Love that places another person's purity and destiny above one's own sexual, romantic and emotional desires. *This* is building in the image of God. Every time we build a relationship according to God's Word, we infuse it with Babel-shattering gospel power.

The Garden Always Wins

Have you ever seen a tree root grow through man-made infrastructure, like concrete or roads? That tree root took its time, but the concrete couldn't stop it. I always feel a little smug, because it reminds me that the Garden will always triumph over Babel. Perhaps not immediately, but Scripture assures us that at the end of our story, at the end of the age, the Garden will prevail. When the rivers of time have dried up, and space and history give way to eternity, God's people won't be in a tower – they'll be in a garden. And in that garden, there'll be this glorious ploughshare: the Tree of Life.

Revelation describes this garden, where stands the "*tree of life*, bearing twelve kinds of fruit and yielding a fresh crop for each month. And the leaves of the tree are for the *healing* of the nations" (Rev 22:2 BSB, emphasis mine). It's no coincidence that our Bibles open and close with a garden. Gardens are our destiny. Fruitfulness is our calling. Healthy relationships are our inheritance.

Did you notice that the *healing* for the nations is attached to this Ploughshare? The relational remedy for this generation is found on the first and last pages of your Bible. You do not need a smartphone to be an influencer when you grasp the gospel. This Ploughshare will profoundly and eternally influence every relationship you have and are yet to have. The gospel is the medicine for the Babel epidemic. Can Jesus heal our broken heart? Absolutely. Can He teach us a better way? You bet. Can He turn poison into promise? That's what He does. If we plough our relationships with the gospel of Christ, I shiver with joyful anticipation to think of what might happen when people step onto the soil of our lives. You've seen tourists flock to observe old ruins; brick-and-mortar towers that once stood tall and proud, that are now wasted away after being subject to the elements for centuries. But this gospel? It's eternal, and it's evergreen.

The Sexual Gospel

You might be wondering why a book on relationships is launching straight into the topic of sex. Surely, it makes more sense to begin with, say, singleness, to proceed to dating, and to eventually work toward sex and marriage. Actually, starting with sex is a pretty scriptural approach, because God starts here, too. It's somewhat amusing that some people think that God doesn't approve of sex, when it's literally the first thing He tells humans to do: "Then God blessed them and said, 'Be fruitful and multiply...'" (Genesis 1:28).

How do you multiply human beings? There's only one way – and it's a great way. I mean, He could have made it an unenjoyable or clinical experience. Apparently God is not a strict pragmatist. He places great value on joy, play, fun, and rest. He even precedes the entire command with His blessing!

Obviously the Kingdom commission to "be fruitful and multiply" extends beyond the idea of physically populating the earth. Genesis 1:28 is more than simply begetting more humans through the act of sex. It is about fruitfully filling the earth with more image-bearers to carry out God's good purposes and steward his good creation. In the New Testament, being "fruitful and multiplying" takes on spiritual connotations when Jesus tells us to "produce much fruit" in the form of disciples (Jn 15:16 & Matt 28:19–20). This mandate of course encompasses single and infertile people who cannot "be fruitful and multiply" in a biological sense.

However, when it comes to our sexual worldview, the crucial point is this: for Adam and Eve, sex was very much a part of being obedient to the first command ever uttered to humanity. While we might gloss over it, I believe it esteems the role of family in the expansion of God's Kingdom. Modern culture is slowly pulling the family unit apart at the seams. In fact, being married and having children is attracting disdain in some quarters of society. Getting hitched and starting a family is sometimes seen as something that holds us back, preventing us from being successful and progressing or "growing." Ironically, growth primarily came *through* family for the ancients in Scripture. Remember when we discussed that the Bible is set in a collectivist society? Family was God's first covenant community, and flesh-and-blood lineage was the means through which He brought the Messiah into the world. The Kingdom came through the Messianic *"Seed"* and you can see how even the language of "seed" connects the redemption of Jesus back to the Garden mandate. Family matters, and so does sex.

Sex is Powerful

So, with all this being said, we know sex is a big deal. We do ourselves no favours if we even entertain notions of otherwise. Secular education trivialises it into a somewhat casual affair, teaching that so long as we don't get pregnant or an STD, there is little other consequence. But even our physiology testifies against that, which we'll explore further in the following chapter.

When we think about it, if an activity has the capacity to produce human life, it's extremely powerful. Not even the angels are allowed the privilege of joining God in the creation of new life, since they are not sexual beings, but *we* reflect our Creator in this remarkable way! (God is not a sexual being, but we image Him in the capacity to create new life, physically and spiritually, populating the earth with children and/or disciples!) I can imagine the celestial beings looking upon us and marvelling, gob smacked by our design. The fact that secular society reduces sex to a one-dimensional experience in the form of one-night stands, flings, or de facto relationships is baffling, because sex is so much better, sacred, and more powerful than that! And hopefully, by the time this book is finished I'll have made the argument that it's completely worth saving for a lifelong binding covenant.

Sexuality is Like Fire

Unless we admit that sex is powerful, we're going to misuse and potentially abuse it. Naturally, we handle powerful things differently. It's the reason we handle a bomb differently to a beachball. Fire is powerful, so we know it has the potential to be both wonderful and dangerous. Inside a home, no one will protest the need for it to be guarded within the boundaries of a fireplace. Within these boundaries, fire brings light, warmth, comfort, and atmosphere to others. But left unguarded? Not only does it have the potential to burn the house down, but to ravage a nation.

As an Australian, I have witnessed firsthand what wildfires can do to a country. In recent years, our country dominated the world news cycle as unguarded flames laid waste to our sunburnt land. Still, we hadn't thought much about fire safety until flames were uncontrollably burning fifteen kilometres away from our houses. All of a sudden we were downloading fire-tracking apps and developing a deep disapproval for any suspected pyromaniacs! No one challenged the strict fire restrictions issued from the Australian government and firefighters. When wildfires reach out-of-control proportions, restrictions are gratefully accepted as a hallmark of communal safety.

Likewise, if we don't guard our sexual habits with boundaries, it does damage not just to ourselves but to other people. Things can quickly escalate into a wildfire that is increasingly difficult to control, ultimately leaving a trail of broken hearts in its wake. Let's not be ignorant to the great and wondrous power of sex. If we realise the power, we'll consider *protecting* that power. Safe within the confines of biblical boundaries, sex is a wonderful, fruitful, life-giving thing – just as God intended it in the beginning.

Tridimensional Beings

The problem with the progressive perspective of sex is it's shallow (lacking depth) and feeble (lacking strength). The Bible readily acknowledges that sex engages every part of our being – mind, body, and spirit. Hollywood culture, on the other hand, reduces it to an activity that exalts pleasure over purpose.

For us to grasp the depth of this, we must dig further into what it really means to be made in the "image of God." God is not tridimensional, since the term applies to things constrained by time, space, and matter, but He is *triune*. He is three-in-one. Since we're made in the image of God, it shouldn't really shock us that we ourselves are tridimensional beings. We're not the same as God, but we're *like* him (Gen 1:26). We are comprised of body, soul, and spirit (1 Thess. 5:23), and you can't really figure out where one ends and the other begins. We're not compartmentalised neatly into a body (a corporeal container), a soul (mind, will, and emotions) and a spirit (the eternal part of us connected to God). It would be easier to understand ourselves if they were three distinctly separate entities to be mathematically observed, measured, and managed. But just as the concept of the Trinity remains much a glorious enigma, so are we! Our body, soul, and spirit are mysteriously interconnected and impossible to be separated from one another. Our heart affects our thoughts. Our thoughts affect our behaviour. Our behaviour affects our thoughts, and our thoughts affect our heart! Perhaps Solomon was considering this connection when he wrote: "Guard your heart above all else, for it determines the course of your life" (Proverbs 4:23).

This tendency to separate what shouldn't be separated is not exclusively a modern practice. While the Apostle Paul was helping pen the New Testament, the Greeks and Romans were busy pitting the body against the soul. Their philosophers would argue that you need to hold the body in contempt and restrain it, while the elites regarded it as merely a pleasure-machine. Either way, their options were either to abuse the body or indulge it, and it was connected directly to their worldview: They believed that once they died, the soul was freed from its bodily prison and wafted up to some sort of heaven.[1] Since the body is destined for destruction, they figured they could do whatever they wanted with it, with their spirit remaining unaffected. As you can imagine, there was little constraint upon sexuality, and young slave girls were the ones who paid the heaviest price at the hands of depraved men.

Thank God the Hebrew worldview was radically different. They read the same creation narrative you and I do, believing their physical bodies were as much a reflection of God as their souls. This is why they (and we) have looked forward to a *bodily* resurrection, not just a spiritual one.² The whole package belongs to God, not just some portion of us. What God's people did with their bodies was directly connected to their spirituality and the opposite was also true – what they believed spiritually was directly connected to what they did with their bodies. They let an ancient truth shape their worldview of sexuality over against the prevailing Hellenistic culture. You and I would be wise to do the same.

Holy Hybrids

Theologians have found fancier language for this, calling us psychosomatic beings, meaning we are fully physical *and* fully spiritual – or what C.S. Lewis would affectionately deem a "*hybrid*."³ These conditions are intrinsically connected and cannot be separated. To say so is to succumb to heresy we can loosely categorize as "Gnosticism" or "materialism".

Gnosticism involves a *dualistic* concept of being human by separating the body from the soul. The soul (or spirit) is prioritised, regarding the body somewhat of an irrelevant burden.⁴ No need to worry so much about honouring your body, addressing physical needs and concrete boundaries. "Feelings" are worshipped over and against physical reality, leading to the belief that what I feel on the *inside* defines the truth, or is most important. This worldview underpins much of the current confusion around identity as people allow how they *feel* to determine who they *are*, over and above concrete truth found in Scripture.

Meanwhile, materialism exalts precisely the opposite. If you can't see it, touch it, or smell it, it's not real or it matters significantly less. It reduces humans to a physical body and nothing more.[5] As you can imagine, a materialistic view of sex reduces humans to two bodies engaging in an activity that has no (or little) moral, emotional or spiritual meaning. Upon this worldview the pornography and sex trafficking industries thrive. The worship of the physical body is inevitable for materialists, and our mind and spirit are burned up on its altar.

Over and against these extremes, our Bible testifies that we are *both* spiritual and physical. Our physicality is what defines us as a creature, not Creator. Our spirituality is what separates us from (and elevates us above) the plants and animals. Why does this matter to you and me? Because this psychosomatic condition is what makes our relationships *unique* in all Creation. We are the prize of Creation because we get to have this special relationship with our Creator and one another. We are indeed, as the psalmist writes, "fearfully and wonderfully made" for the express purpose of imaging God to the world around us (Psalm 139:14).

Sex is Spiritual

This is particularly important when applied to sexuality. The world tends to categorise sex as exclusively physical, but Scripture testifies that it is also utterly spiritual.

Hebrews 13:4 tells us to "Honour marriage, and guard the sacredness of sexual intimacy between wife and husband" (MSG). The word "sacred," as used by Eugene Peterson in *The Message* paraphrase, means to be connected with God or dedicated for a religious purpose. Wait, sex is ... godly? Absolutely. At risk of stating the obvious, *anything* God invents is *god-ly*. It wasn't an accident when He instilled us with a sex drive. But, as with most good gifts, He also sovereignly ordained a time, a place, and a context within which it should be unwrapped. He did this to ensure both our joy and protection. Great gifts require great stewardship and taking time to steward a sex drive before engaging the ignition is extremely beneficial for us. He gave it before we could use it, so we learn the art of stewarding some*thing* precious before giving it away to some*one* precious.

Yet for some, it's difficult to think of sex as *holy, beautiful, moral,* and *good*. Surely those things belong in the "spiritual box," and sex belongs in a "physical box," right? Actually, sexuality is tridimensional because *we* are. It involves every part of us – body, soul, and spirit. Pulling them apart goes against our very nature, whether we choose to believe it or not.

I'm sure some reading this have had the displeasure of putting together a piece of furniture of Swedish origin. You know the kind – with a million nuts and bolts, random pieces, and a booklet of illegible instructions. Think about sexuality this way: Let's say we've put together a chair. The chair has a purpose (to be sat in, obviously). But say we decide to pull it apart again. Do we still have a chair to sit on? No … we have the bits and pieces that make up a chair, but now they're separated out, and when pulled apart, they can't perform the purpose for which they were made. It is the same with sex: If we attempt to pull it apart, tearing the physical from the emotional from the spiritual, then we're not left with sex. We're left with a dismantled version of it, and it won't perform the purpose for which it was made. We'll get a piece of it, but not the purpose. I believe this accounts for much of the aching hearts that result from misused sexuality. Sex has ceased to be what it was purposed to be: a mysterious means by which we would be fruitful and multiply; a joyful medium through which we would express a sacred covenant oneness. It's not performing the spiritual, emotional, and physical purpose for which it was gloriously ordained. We're not sitting in chairs, so to speak. We're on the floor, holding up pieces while we wipe our tears and scroll for more ideas.

The Founding Fathers of Sexual Depravity

As Western society moves away from biblical origins, people are not only deconstructing and reconstructing their faith, they are deconstructing and reconstructing ideas around sexual morality. It is notable that much of the trending sexual ethic can be traced back to Friedrich Nietzsche (1844–1900) whose philosophy was that God was dead and therefore there was no such thing as absolute truth or absolute morals. He claimed Christianity was oppressive, restricting the "unlimited freedom" of society.[6] Sigmund Freud (1856–1939) known as the Founder of Modern Psychology, followed in Nietzsche's footsteps. He too believed religion to be a human construct, regarding humans as highly developed animals. His sexual worldview was that sex was purely physical, with no spiritual or moral criteria attached.[7] We'll discuss below how this viewpoint results in a downward spiral that leads to injury and death of the innocent. Horrifically, he believed children were not innocent, but rather have sexual desires (including infants). Finally, we come to Father of the Sexual Revolution, the infamous Alfred Kinsey (1894–1956). Kinsey was a Harvard-educated zoologist who's infamous *"Kinsey Reports"* deceived the public into thinking it was "common" to engage in sexually immoral behaviour, including sex with animals, marital affairs, masturbation, and more. He did this by using his famous sex interviews at a time when television was a relatively new phenomenon and regarded as a major source of authority. His research made normal people feel like a foolish minority for ascribing to monogamous marriage. However, later his reports were found to be fraudulent. Kinsey had purposely selected the likes of prisoners, rapists, ex-cons, paedophiles, and prostitutes for his interviews, presenting them as the "norm" to manipulate the sexual worldview of the public. However, it was too late. The way his false reports impacted society has been paralleled to that of when the atomic bomb was introduced, opening the door to what is known as the "sexual revolution" of the 1960s, better known as the "summer of love."[8] However, a more accurate label would be the "summer of sexual depravity." These men changed the way many thought and still think about sexual morality and sexual ethics, and we must be very cautious to accept all the information and philosophies that trickle down to us from so-called authorities in this space.

The Quicksand Spiral

As much as evolutionary theories attempt to throw humans and animals in the same bucket, we approach sex (and are affected by it) very differently to animals. Humans and animals may have been created on the same day, but when God presented Eve to Adam, he sure knew there was a difference! The fact that our sexuality is spiritual is what separates us from the animals, who have sex on instinct. Animals don't "make love" and humans don't "breed," so to speak. Humans are able to engage their hearts, emotions and morality in sex, and it's part of what makes us special creatures. However, if we do separate sex from the spiritual, we tragically become *animalistic* in our approach. Genesis reveals to us that humans are curious beings, entirely set apart from the animals and instilled with a volitional and moral nature. The secular theory of Evolution, on the other hand, teaches us that we are no more than glorified primates who are subject to our biological and carnal desires.

When sex is reduced to a physical experience alone, we become driven by instinct, hormones, and desire. They're great for the backseat but make terrible drivers, just so you know! When we elevate how we *feel* above what is right and moral, we're guided according to what gives us most pleasure. But as countless love songs have testified throughout history, pleasure quickly turns into pain if it is not tethered to moral and spiritual accountability. Cue the downward spiral into sensual quicksand.

If we're led by instinct alone, humans eventually become like objects to be used instead of image-bearers with hearts and destinies. Relationships become self-centred in nature, motivated by gratification and what (or who) makes *me* happy. What (or who) makes *me* feel good. What (or who) makes *me* feel satisfied. And because no human can wholly fulfil that need (only God) we tend to recycle people, leading to casual flings and relationships void of commitment and honour of the other person. We think that because they're not making us feel what we want to feel, it must mean we need to move on to the next person and see if *they* measure up. The "try before you buy" slogan of mass consumerism has infected our approach to relationships. We don't just shop for objects; we shop for people. The self-satisfying world of Babel offers us plenty of retail therapy any time we want it, chanting *"Shop till you drop!"* with every online dating profile.

Once we've objectified people, the quicksand sucks us down further. When people become objects to us, we conclude that we can sell and exchange them. This is literally what fuels the pornography and prostitution industry. People in these industries have become sexual objects – objects to be sold in exchange for money, and a lot of money at that (over 90 billion dollars a year if you were wondering.[9])

And guess what the pornography industry drives? It is one of the leading influencers of human sex trafficking, where people are stolen, abused, and exchanged for money to powerful, wealthy people. People who concluded that partners can be reduced to objects, sex can be reduced to pleasure, and humanity can be reduced to brutish beasts.

And finally, if we can sell and exchange people, it's only natural to surmise we can also get rid of them. Sexual activity has consequences, and among many variables, pregnancy can be one of them. A baby should never be an unfortunate *consequence* of sex; children were always supposed to be a celebrated *blessing* of sex. But if we've had sex outside of the safety of marriage and are surprised by pregnancy, rather than carry the weight of the choice we made when we climbed into bed, society tells us we can dispose of him or her. Before we play the blame game on one particular generation or another, even the ancient Romans didn't regard children as humans until the father decided to own them. Day-old baby girls were regularly dumped in the streets to the point of clogging the sewers.[10] One of the reasons the early Church grew so rapidly was not only because we outbred the Roman empire, but because the Church population naturally increased through adoption. Early Christians valued life, family and children over and against the cultural tide of convenience and human expediency – because they believed to *"be fruitful and multiply"* was both a spiritual and physical Kingdom mandate. It still is.

We can wind back the clock further and further, but we'll still find some form of the downward spiral illustrated above in every period of history – and we'll follow the toxic root system all the way back to Genesis 3. Friends, this is what happens when humanity reduces sex to a purely physical experience. It quite literally dehumanises people. And nine times out of ten, this is what makes us think sex is a "dirty word." It becomes taboo because of its association with shame, regret, or an uneasy feeling we can't quite pin down, yet we know we've somehow gone against the grain of our being. But remember: Something is only dirty if you cast it in the dirt. The truth is, sex is a wonderful gift from God!

Sex is Good

Sex is not dirty. It's a crucial part of what makes us human.

Anything and everything God creates is inherently good. In Genesis 1 we hear the repeated proclamation over His creation like an anthem of truth, *"It was good."* This means if God came up with the idea for humans to have sex, it has to be intrinsically *good*. It is good for us, it will bless us, it will bring life and vitality and enjoyment to us. It is good for our body and our mind and our soul (science affirms this). It's given to us in a safe context called marriage which protects not only us from being used and abandoned, but any potential children who might be born from that relationship.

Now, here's where it gets complicated: The Enemy cannot create anything, he can only corrupt. Much to his dismay, creation is just not in his wheelhouse. So, he takes God's good creation and presents to us a perverted version of it, hoping we'll take the bait. Anything to short-change us, right? This is because he is anti-life. Anti-fruit. Anti-garden. In leu of sexual wholeness, he entices us with sexual blessing without sexual commitment. Pornography, casual sex, and sexual relationships outside of marriage provide sensual *pleasure* without commitment to a *person*. If we're willing to ride the downward spiral, it opens up the most extreme possibilities: prostitution, bestiality, sexual abuse, and (as we read above) death. Now death – *that's* in his wheelhouse. That's his endgame. According to Jesus in John 10:10 "The thief's purpose is to steal and kill and destroy. My purpose is to give them a rich and satisfying life."

Dear friends, we don't need to opt for the perverted version of sex. We're not borrowing the idea of sex and relationships from the world and trying to "Christianise" it or "purify" it so it feels more appropriate. No, *God* came up with the whole idea. As with all genius engineers, He has a monopoly on how it works best. He has purposed it to bring us life, health, blessing, and fruitfulness, if we figure out how to do it according to the engineering instructions. It's time we resisted settling for that serpent's scraps and rediscover the original, unsoiled idea.

Sex was never meant to bring shame, regret, or pain. It is meant to be safe, wholesome, and intimate. For it to be this way, it has to involve more than just our bodies – it must involve our minds, intellect, emotions, and spirit. I love the particular language used in *The Message* to paraphrase Paul dropping some exquisite sexual theology in 1 Cor 6:16–20:

"There's more to sex than mere skin on skin. Sex is as much spiritual mystery as physical fact. As written in Scripture, "The two become one." Since we want to become spiritually one with the Master, we must not pursue the kind of sex that avoids commitment and intimacy, leaving us more lonely than ever – the kind of sex that can never "become one." There is a sense in which sexual sins are different from all others. In sexual sin *we violate the sacredness of our own bodies*, these bodies that were made for God-given and God-modelled love, for "becoming one" with another. Or didn't you realise that your body is a sacred place, the place of the Holy Spirit? Don't you see that you can't live however you please, squandering what God paid such a high price for? *The physical part of you is not some piece of property belonging to the spiritual part of you*. God owns the whole works. So let people see God in and through your body" (MSG; emphasis mine).

Before you let the Lizard wreak shame and send you running for fig leaves again, I want to remind you that Paul isn't penning this letter to either pagans or virgins. He was writing to people who had most definitely strayed from the Garden path in their past. People who, according to his own words in verses 9–11, "use and abuse each other, use and abuse sex, use and abuse the earth and everything in it, don't qualify as citizens in God's kingdom. A number of you know from experience what I'm talking about, for *not so long ago you were on that list …*" (MSG; emphasis mine).

They were relatively fresh Christians who had been born into, and swept up in, a Hellenistic culture of sexual chaos.

Paul continues, "Since then, you've been cleaned up and given a fresh start by Jesus, our Master, our Messiah, and by our God present in us, the Spirit" (1 Cor 6:11 MSG). There's no room for condemnation between the words found in Scripture. If you need a fresh start, you won't get it from the world, but you'll definitely get it from Jesus. Time, as it turns out, doesn't heal all wounds. No amount of minutes, meditation, or fragrant body wash will clean us up when we've stuffed it up – it's the Holy Spirit alone who carries this medicine of mercy: "*God present in us.*"

Botox or Bible?

As Christians, we believe the truth is firmly planted in the Garden of Eden: every human is made in the image of God. This same God also ascribes every human with unchanging worth, dignity, purpose, and identity over and above painful circumstances, discontented feelings, and confusion. This flies in the face of the noisy messages that come from the cosmetic beauty industries, pornography websites, advertising campaigns and Avant guard influencers. While they relentlessly exhort us to change our physical form, filter our faces and inflate our bodies with silicon to keep up with the "reality TV" stars, God already gave us a part of the body that can be transformed. Ironically, it can't be seen from the outside, but it's so powerful that it tells the rest of the body what to do. According to the Bible, the brain is reshaped by changing the mind – or as Paul writes: "be transformed by the renewing of your mind" (Rom 12:2, NIV). The great power of the gospel is that upon salvation we are given "the mind of Christ" (1 Cor 2:16). This gives great hope to those who have a distorted and confused perspective about themselves. To the anorexic whose internal feelings do not match up with his or her exterior, there is hope for healing. To those who suffer low self-esteem and self-hatred, there is hope for contentment. To those who ache from a deep sense of rejection, there is hope for acceptance. While Babel offers us liposuction, Botox, selfies and social media hacks, the Bible offers us worth, dignity, acceptance, and a hope that is anchored in transformation – in the present life, but most importantly, the eternal life to come.

For this reason, according to Paul, "the body is the Lord's" and we can bring him glory with what we do (or don't do) with it. Remember, Jesus honoured us with His body when He died in it. And regardless of what we've done with ours, He secured our dignity when He rose in His. Body, mind, and spirit: Every inch of us is treasured by our Creator. Guard yourself from ideology that wants to suck you down into a sensual quagmire. Steel yourself against the cultural tide that presents a soiled version of something pure, precious, and powerful. It's time to go *with* the grain of our design, not against it. Turn the page with me and let's investigate what this truly means.

Biology Theology

We've explored how sex is a tridimensional experience, involving our body, our soul, and our spirit. We might attempt to separate sexuality from our soul and spirit, but our biology works against us in this regard. What we do with our body is always going to be connected to our soul, and this is because God is *for* us, not against us. He's rigged the system so that when we marry someone, we can maintain a connection with them through all the shifting seasons of life. He came up with marvellous Super Glue to help bind us together: Sex. Yes, sex is like Super Glue. When we engage in sexual activity, there's an undeniable bond that takes place. Not so many will argue with this. But what is interesting is that if we measure the levels of hormones that help create this bond, they drop every time we change sexual partners. In simple terms: The more lovers we take, the less sticky (for want of a better word) the bond we make.

Sex is Like Super Glue

It's like when you put one of those strong, hospital-grade Band-Aids on your skin. It sticks really well the first time, so that when you rip it off it takes bits of skin and a whole bunch of hairs with it. It also really *hurts,* speaking from personal experience! But let's say you try and apply that same Band-Aid again. It might stick, but some of that adhesive has come off, so it won't grip on quite as firmly. Every time you repeat this process more adhesive is removed and the Band-Aid gets less and less sticky until eventually, well, it doesn't stick at all. Likewise, sex is a powerful adhesive and the first time we break away from someone we've had sex with will be the most painful and memorable experience. But when we engage in sexual activity over and over with different partners, the bond created becomes less and less permanent until eventually it can feel meaningless.[1] Sex addicts will testify to this phenomenon. And if sex feels meaningless, people begin to do weirder things in an attempt to *make* it meaningful and achieve satisfaction. (Adult shops, sex toy manufacturers, and the 19-billion-dollar porn industry certainly aren't complaining about this dysfunction.)

The reason we can't separate body and soul is because whenever we engage in sexual activity of any kind, hormones are going to be released in our bodies that affect the soul realm (the mind, will, and emotions). Regardless of our ideology, our background, or our reasoning, we can't stop our body from doing what it's designed to do. We are marvellously complex, and according to Psalm 139, it's a complexity that glorifies God: "You made all the delicate, inner parts of my body and knit me together in my mother's womb. Thank you for making me so wonderfully complex! Your workmanship is marvellous – how well I know it" (v13–14).

Created for Commitment

So how exactly does this proverbial "glue" work? It's different for men and women. For women, one of the major hormones released in sexual activity is *oxytocin*. Oxytocin is known as the "cuddle hormone" or "love hormone"[2] and for good reason: It's an extremely potent bonding neurochemical allowing a woman to attach herself to the most meaningful people in her world. It creates feelings of warmth, trust, closeness, and selfless concern for the wellbeing of the one she has bonded to.[3] It's also a common word heard around the maternity wards: not only is it released during sex, but it stimulates contractions during childbirth, milk production for breastfeeding, and is the main hormone that promotes infant-mother bonding in those crucial early days. Oxytocin absolutely surges when a woman has a baby to ensure she is bonded to that baby and promotes a willingness to sacrifice herself for him or her.[4] Simply put, those hormones are released in copious amounts to bond her to someone for *life*, not a temporary interest.

The guys don't miss out on the cuddle hormones altogether though – it's released in both men and women during positive physical contact, like hugging for extended periods of time. It floods a father's brain when he holds his newborn.[5] (Which explains why, when my husband held our newborn daughter in adoration for three hours, he still claims only three minutes had passed!)

However, for the men, the primary hormone released during sex is *vasopressin*. This neurochemical causes a man to bond to a woman he has intimate physical interaction with. Some call it the "commitment hormone" or "monogamy molecule" (monogamy meaning having one partner) since it promotes long term commitment, loyalty, increased attachment, and attention. It also creates that "jealous" tendency that most of us have seen break out in pub brawls or high school corridors. Before we nod and roll our eyes, there is actually a holy context for jealousy – even God claims to love his people with a "jealous love." It means that because God loves us, He demands exclusivity of worship in the same way a husband should demand exclusivity from his wife (and vice versa). If a husband didn't care that his wife was unfaithful, how could he truly love her? The reason most of us are not ok with our spouses having affairs and multiple partners is *because* we love them. Married love is a privileged and exclusive love.

A man's brain is inundated with vasopressin during sex, creating a bond with every woman he has sexual interaction with no matter who they are (or what they look like!) And just like oxytocin, vasopressin not only promotes bonding between sexual partners, but bonding between father and child.[6] Atheist scientists might scratch their heads at this amazing design, since the theory of evolution has no need for sexual morality or monogamy, but rather relies on the idea of having as many sexual "mates" to ensure genes are passed on. On the other hand, Scripture unapologetically answers the question of why we're made this way. Whether we're talking about sex or family: we're created for covenant, so He built us to bond.

Now the third set of primary hormones released during sex are endorphins, and most of us are already familiar with these. We affectionately nickname them "happy hormones" or "feel-good chemicals" since they boost happiness, causing the person to feel calm, secure, and even a sense of euphoria. Oh, and they're also the body's natural painkiller.[7] Great idea God! There are many activities that can give us the euphoric high from endorphins, such as laughing or running (this is what is known as the "runner's high.") It's no wonder endorphins can be highly addictive. People want to experience the rush again and again, and it's no different when it comes to sex.

Whether it's a casual fling or our wedding night, our bodies will connect our body to our soul. They file these intense intimate experiences away in our sexual memory, which is why breakups hurt and exes are difficult to forget, even by the most seasoned serial lovers.

The Counterfeit of Sexual Blessing

Contrary to popular opinion, it's the Devil who hates sex, not God. The Devil hates sex because he hates life and blessing, and he knows sex brings connection that both expresses and generates life and blessing. As we have realised, he cannot create, but he *can* counterfeit. Have you ever seen counterfeit money? At a quick glance it looks and even feels the same as real money. But upon a closer inspection, the trained eye will spot the difference. Fake money isn't worth anything, so it can't buy you anything, and you end up with nothing.

How do I know money is authentic and not a counterfeit? I have to hold it up to the light and look closely. If it's fake money, it'll be exposed, because only authentic currency is stamped with the hologram of the Australian coat of arms, and it is only seen under the light. There's a lot of fake versions of sexuality circulating out there. More than ever, we need to hold sexuality up to the light of God's truth. When we do, lustful sexuality is exposed for what it is: shallow and selfish. Authentic sexuality is stamped with the approval and blessing of God, and it's authenticated with covenant commitment.

Lust is the Devil's *counterfeit* of sexual blessing. Let's just call it for what it is: sex that is fuelled by lust is not real sex, it's fake. If we inspect it closely and peel back the curtains of people's lives, we see that it yields pain, shame, and brokenness. It doesn't carry the worth or dignity of the real thing, and if you try to spend it, you'll wind up sexually bankrupt. In other words, it's not worth anything, so it can't buy us blessing, and we end up with nothing but heartache.

Selfish Sexuality

Lust is driven by the uncontrolled desire to satisfy the self *outside* of God's boundaries and will. This is where Hollywood and humanism meet and eagerly shake hands. As they say, "sex sells" – but not so much when it's tethered to the concepts of abstinence and faithfulness! Sexual humanism attempts to plunder sexual blessing without the selflessness, sacrifice, and commitment that a covenant relationship requires. The overall message being celebrated and promoted from the pulpit of pop culture is *"Let's take a shortcut. Let's have sex without intimacy. Sex without commitment! Even sex without ... a person!"*

Self-centred sex climaxes (forgive the pun) in pornography, providing sexual stimulation without having to honour, pursue, or meet the needs of anyone else but "me." Sex is supposed to involve knowing and being intimately known by another image-bearer. Lust is a parody of sexual blessing and not even close to the real thing. Our digital age has simply made it easier to fall for this counterfeit sexual fulfillment and label it as "normal." Trust me, this is one shortcut that won't take you where you want to go. Forget the garden path – it'll take you to the top floor of the Babel tower and bring you crashing down.

Just like eating junk food all day ruins your appetite, porn destroys your sexual appetite. Think about it this way: If your diet consists of junk food, you won't crave a healthy home-cooked meal. Your appetite tends to be shaped according to what you feed it (more on this in the chapter titled *"Babel's Table"*). If you're hooked on sugar, salt, and flavour enhancers like MSG, they eventually become the only things that will satisfy. And you'll need more and more of them to gratify your increasingly uncontrolled cravings.

Whether we're talking about food or sex, our appetites operate based on similar principles. Feeding on porn will train your brain for unrealistic sexual experiences and excessive stimulation. By the time you step up to the altar or climb into bed with your spouse, you won't be hungry for the real thing. You'll need extreme stimulation to satisfy a ferocious appetite awakened by lust. Instead of viewing your spouse as a sacred image-bearer, your brain will have been trained to view them as a porn star in the bedroom. Study has shown that the dopamine hit from porn operates in a very similar way to narcotics. The excessive stimulation (via your eyes and hands) results in reduced capacity. Meaning, you build up a tolerance to it and need more and more to get the same result.[8] This makes for a terrible sex life and a huge turn off. Babel attempts to spoon-feed our generation these sexual narcotics and many are quite literally addicted by the time they say, "I do."

Needless to say, pornography is destroying marriages before they've even begun. It's like expecting an Olympic marathon runner to smoke and drink heavily and still win a trophy at the end of the race. Marriage is a marathon: a lifelong commitment. God wants us to win gold, but a generation drunk on lust and inhaling sexual stimulants will not – and are not – making it to the finish line. If the eyes are the window to the soul, then our generation is corrupting the soul faster than our thumbs can scroll.

Jesus provides us sober commentary on this profound connection between body and soul in Matthew 5:27–28: "You have heard the commandment that says, 'You must not commit adultery.' But I say, anyone who even *looks at* a woman with lust has already committed adultery with her in his *heart*" (emphasis mine).

Essentially, He is articulating what we've been discovering: You can't separate your body from your soul. The eye is a part of the physical body and what (or who) we look at plays a huge role in the health of our heart. In verse 29 we're shown the cost of sexual purity in a lust-crazed culture: "So if your eye – even your good eye – causes you to lust, gouge it out and throw it away."

According to our Saviour, we're better off being blind than using our eyes for sexual perversion. When Jesus walked the planet, you had to cover your eyes from prostitutes as you strolled the streets. In our day, we have to do the same as we scroll our feeds. We're better off smashing our phones than corrupting our souls. *The Message* paraphrases Matthew 5:27–28 this way: "Let's not pretend this is easier than it really is. If you want to live a morally pure life, here's what you have to do: You have to blind your right eye the moment you catch it in a lustful leer" (MSG).

Jesus is revealing the radical cost of following Him – that's why He calls us to count it before committing to it.[9] But if it's any consolation to you, there is a price tag to either path you choose. Moral purity does involve sacrifice, but the benefits of sexual blessing far outweigh the cost. If we refuse the lustful "snacks" that rob us of a healthy appetite, we'll be ravenous for dinner and cherish every mouthful.

Isaiah 55:2 says "Why do you spend your money on junk food, your hard-earned cash on cotton candy? Listen to me, listen well: Eat only the best, fill yourself with only the finest" (MSG). All are welcome to dine at the table of sexual blessing, but there are no shortcuts to your seat. At the end of the day, counterfeit money can't pay for a thing, and counterfeit sex can't buy you a seat at the table. Christian worldview aside, if you're looking for the easiest way to get there, it's saving sex until marriage. Forget morality and spirituality for a moment. Forget the fact that the people in those erotic images are image-bearers in whom God has instilled worth and awaits them to repent and reclaim their dignity. Let's look at this purely from a physical and emotional perspective for your personal health: If you want to know the best (and most pain-free) way to have a healthy and fulfilling sex life, it's to wait until you're married. In this case, waiting is not a sacrifice – it's just a really smart investment.

Selfless Sexuality

Here is the good news: If we're talking about the *cost* of sin (sexual or otherwise) we can be assured Christ has paid it and made it possible to redeem what has been lost, including our sexual wholeness. There's simply no room for hopelessness when we talk about the gospel of Jesus Christ. Sometimes we're numb to the truth, but sin hurts us, and sexual sin *especially* hurts. But it's our sin that shows just how extraordinary the gospel really is. He makes possible what should not be possible. It's more than paying our moral debt for getting into Heaven – it's giving us His Spirit who shapes our lives, so we don't have to live in a way that earns us hurt, shame, and ugliness.

In God's Kingdom there is always an opportunity to do what is right for when we get it wrong. We can un-train our brain, renew our mind, and relearn purity through a process called "sanctification." Our stories might have begun in heartache, but they don't have to end in it. But I repeat, there are no shortcuts here. Babel wants blessing fast and wants it *now*. But if you want the real thing, you might need to clear out some rubble and re-landscape the yard before you sow new seeds. We'll delve further into this process in our final chapter "Breaking Up with Babel," but for now, let's consider the power of exclusivity when it comes to sexual blessing.

God has ordained sex to take place in an exclusive, monogamous, binding relationship called a "covenant." This relationship requires not only lifelong commitment, but a continual laying down of ourselves for one another. Ephesians 5:25–29 lays out some outstanding relationship theology:

"For husbands, this means love your wives, just as Christ loved the church. He gave up his life for her ... to make her holy and clean, washed by the cleansing of God's word ... In the same way, husbands ought to love their wives as they love their own bodies. For a man who loves his wife actually shows love for himself. No one hates his own body but feeds and cares for it, just as Christ cares for the church."

Now, before we engage in the Battle of the Sexes, note that Paul carefully prefaces everything he is about to say with a stunning statement of equality: "Submit to one another out of reverence to Christ" (Eph 5:21). He then addresses wives specifically to "submit to your husbands ..." (v22) but he doesn't spend much more time here since by Roman law, they had to do that anyway. Thank you, Captain Obvious. But for men to do likewise was a *much* more radical proposal in Roman antiquity. This is why Paul spills more ink urging husbands to also lay their lives down in a deeply sacrificial way, since wives were already culturally obligated to do so. This special brand of submission is mutual, others-honouring and free from power-play and exploitation. Paul's emphasis is a marital oneness and unity that radically images the gospel to a watching world.[10] May our relationships do the same.

Rather than getting lost down the rabbit hole of pitting Complementarians against Egalitarians,[11] let's come back to the reason you're reading this chapter. Among many things,

Paul reveals a profound truth embedded in every successful marriage: serving your spouse is serving *you*. Blessing them is blessing *you*. Their joy is *your* joy. And sexual intimacy is a beautiful expression of this covenant oneness: putting their needs before your own. Sexual intimacy was never meant to be the giving of yourself for the sake of your*self*, but the yielding of yourself to another in a private setting, charged with sacred mystery and trust, that results in both parties being blessed.

In the beginning, God made *one* flesh into *two*. He pulled Eve from Adam's side. In marriage there is a death of sorts as *two* become *one* flesh. Do you see the beauty? The only way to become "one" is the dying of self in order to serve another. Sexual intimacy is a striking expression of this profound truth. It is a Sexual Gospel: a receiving of blessing that is attained through the giving of the self. Two become one in the most winsome way. And you could not get any further from our quicksand-culture of self-indulgent and selfish sensuality.

Biology and Theology

Hollywood works overtime to convince us that sex on the first date, friends with benefits, multiple sex partners and marital affairs are normal and even acceptable. Screens have desensitised and reshaped what is customary. To be sure, what would have shocked us even one generation ago now merely makes us shrug. While media heralds this so-called sexual "freedom" as normal, our bodies will refuse to cooperate. We must never confuse commonality for normality. What is common for trending culture, as it turns out, is not normal for the body. We can keep up with popular ideals, but our bonding hormones begin to go on strike, because it is decidedly *not* normal. One day, when couples decide it's time to get hitched, many are finding that those bonding chemicals are halfway into retirement. And we're wondering why the divorce rate has risen along with its progeny: heartbreak, insecurity, poor mental health and identity crises.

The Bible says, "Let your wife be a fountain of blessing for you. Rejoice in the wife of your youth" (Proverbs 5:18). You see, God has rigged the system so that your *one* spouse will be a fountain of sexual blessing (and a reason to shout "Hallelujah!") The person you marry in your youth will still be a blessing in the bedroom when you have more wrinkles and your lower back hurts all the time. The parody of perversion will never match the power of exclusivity. You and I are made for it.

It's not difficult to see that our biology aligns with theology. Our hormonal superglue strengthens the binding covenant that is designed to hold two people together for life. We can be held together and remain faithful even when the days get hard, the dishes are piled high, the kids are fuelling your sleep-deprivation and work is stressful. If we come back to the Garden, we'll see that relationships have changing seasons. They're not static, mechanical things we can manufacture like bricks and mortar. To borrow the words of a dear friend, relationships are "not mechanic, they're organic!" As they go through seasons, they grow, wither, and require pruning and tending. God in His infinite wisdom has designed us so when we have chosen "the one" we'll stick with them through thick and thin, winter and spring, youth and old age – till death do us part.

When Two Become One

Hopefully by now we've recognised the bottom line: Sex is super powerful, and it has to be, because it's supposed to hold two people together for a lifetime. In chapter 2 we discussed how sex is like fire, being both potentially wonderful and potentially dangerous. The biblical "fireplace" for sexuality to be expressed is marriage, which harnesses the power of sex to not only bring warmth and wonder, but protection from getting burned. Why does God command us to wait until marriage specifically though?

Why not simply a committed long-term relationship? According to Scripture, the only thing that protects an apparently committed relationship from becoming *un*committed is unbreakable covenant.[1] Even for people in a committed loving relationship, their living together, sharing a dog, buying a dish rack, or having sex doesn't secure that commitment. *Covenant* secures that commitment. If we're as committed as we say, we prove it by our willingness to lay our lives down for one another, sharing our bank accounts, our living quarters, our families, our bodies, and our whole lives in binding vows – we get married. We don't cease sharing our lives when our feelings don't match up with our commitment. We don't back out if we go bankrupt or become ill. To counter the argument that this is too high a demand from an individual, we might consider that the legal age to enlist in the military is eighteen years old. We don't culturally recoil at the concept of an eighteen-year-old committing to lay their life down for their nation, yet we choke on the idea of them doing it for an individual in marriage. Abstinence is completely possible for a young person prior to marriage, and so is lifelong faithfulness afterward. In fact, as we just read in chapter 3, our biology aligns with our theology and greatly helps us in this regard.

When God told Adam and Eve to be fruitful and multiply (have sex) they were in covenant with God and with one another. In other words, Adam and Eve were married when God issued His first glorious command. Genesis 2:24 refers to this when it says "That is why a man leaves his father and mother and is united to his wife, and they become one flesh" (NIV).

The word "united" is the Hebrew *"dabaq"* (דחי) which is a term of covenant exclusivity.[2] As you can see, being "united" also involves sharing living quarters with his new spouse, to begin a *new* covenant community (family). For this reason, we don't live with romantic partners before marriage. It might feel exciting or even seem practical, but inverting God's order has never served us well. Living together is meant to be the outworking of becoming "one flesh" in covenant, and sharing a home beforehand only sets us up for moral compromise. In a sense, the couple sharing a living quarters functions like they're married, without having actually followed through with binding wedding vows.

Much More Than a Piece of Paper

To realise why sex is a sacred act specifically preserved for marriage, we must understand more about covenant. Covenant, it seems, is becoming a foreign word these days, but it was once written into the very fabric of ancient society and still entirely relevant to you and I. In fact, our whole Bible is split into two overarching covenants (we use the word *testaments*). So entrenched was the concept of covenant that the ancients regarded it as higher than Law.[3] Hang on for this history lesson please, because by the end of this chapter we might make sense of the wedding traditions we continue to uphold today. If we can define covenant, we'll be able to properly define what marriage is, what weddings are, and most importantly, the "why" behind the wait when it comes to sex!

In its most basic form, a covenant is a sacred and unbreakable bond between two parties, sealed with legal and ceremonial rites.[4] You may not realise this, but your Bible is telling the story of *covenant* between God and humanity. There are six major covenants that make up our Old Testament which are interconnected and build upon one another before coming to complete fruition in the seventh and final covenant, which is what we call the "*new* covenant" or the *New* Testament![5]

The seven aforementioned covenants and their representatives are as follows:

- 1st: Edenic Covenant – the covenant humankind were created in with God, in the Garden of Eden (Adam)
- 2nd: Adamic Covenant – the covenant God renewed in the Garden after The Fall (Adam)
- 3rd: Noahic Covenant – the covenant God made with all the earth (Noah)
- 4th: Abrahamic Covenant – the covenant God made with a father (Abraham)
- 5th: Mosaic Covenant – the covenant God made with a nation (Moses)
- 6th: Davidic Covenant – the covenant God made with a king (David)
- 7th: The Everlasting Covenant – transcending the previous six and bringing them into fruition (Jesus)[6]

Now here's where it gets *really* interesting. To make (or to use technical terms, *"cut"*) covenant you had to have several things in place, which people in ancient cultures knew very well. Once I mention them, you'll probably be able to spot some of them in Scripture:

Exchanging of coats. This indicates a sharing of bank accounts or the concept of "what's mine is yours." For example, you might notice this exchange when Jonathon transfers the kingdom of Saul to David by cutting covenant (1 Sam 18:3–4).[7]

Exchanging of weapons. This symbolises a sharing of defence and protection. David and Jonathon also exchange swords in covenantal procedure (1 Sam 18:4).

Exchanging of names. They'd take part of one name and insert it into the other. This is why the first man is called *adam* in Hebrew, meaning "human." But when Eve is presented, suddenly the word "man" in Hebrew changes to *ish* (אִישׁ)[8] and she is called *ishshah* (אִשָּׁה).[9] His name is taken and inserted into hers through marriage covenant, poetically exclaimed by Adam with the words *"bone of my bone, flesh of my flesh!"* They are now Man and Wo-man!

Blood cutting. This was usually a mark on your arm. The ancients knew that the only way back to God was bloodshed. Which, by the way, is why an animal had to be killed in the Garden of Eden. God isn't a fan of fashionable fur, but blood must be shed to cover our sin. Bloodshed would seal the covenant and eventually Jesus would take the place of that animal on the cross.[10]

Splitting of an animal. You had to chop it up and walk between the pieces in the eternity symbol. The death of the animal was supposed to be an image of what would happen to you if you were unfaithful to the covenant.[11] In other words it meant "I will die before I am unfaithful to you." You might remember this curious ceremony from Genesis 15.

Declaration of an oath. This outlined all the blessings and the curses attached to the covenant; blessings for keeping it, curses for breaking it. It's exactly what Moses is doing, for example, during his famous "Choose life or death!" speech in Deuteronomy.[12]

Sign of the covenant. Every covenant had a sign to outwardly express that covenant. Noah's covenant sign was a rainbow, Abraham's sign was circumcision, Moses' sign was the Sabbath, and David's sign was having a king on his throne.[13]

Covenant meal. A meal was shared to ratify (validate) the covenant. For example, the Passover was a covenant meal a whole nation was invited to (Exodus 12).[14]

Covenant witness. A witness was designated to watch over the covenant to ensure both parties were faithful. Their job was to announce when one party was unfaithful and it's exactly why the Old Testament prophets are often cranky! The reason they can be so depressing to read is because they're announcing broken covenant as designated witnesses over Israel's covenant with God.[15]

Our entire Christian experience, relationship and belief system revolves around a *covenant* with God. It differs from human marriage in that it's a one-way deal, because we can't actually offer God anything from our side of the bargain. But God has covenanted to enter us into his *protection* (exchanging of coats), his *bank account* (we enter into the riches of His grace), his *name* (we take Christ's name and insert it into our own, calling ourselves *Christ*ians). *Blood cutting* is the most sobering part of Good Friday, Christ symbolically becoming the *animal split into pieces* by dying for us on the cross and his blood sealing the covenant. We are freed from the *curses* of broken covenant (sin) and inherit the *blessings* of God (grace) through Christ. We celebrate and remember this with a *covenant meal* called "communion." We also have a *"sign"* of our covenant, which is the baptism of the Holy Spirit. Our covenant *witness* who keeps watch over this covenant, convicting us when we break it and affirming us when we keep it, is the prophetic voice of God or what we call the Holy Spirit *witness*. Have you ever wondered why Jesus carries his scars into eternity? Christ is our "blood brother" who carries the *mark* of covenant; His scars are the seal of blood covenant held in his body, eternally testifying of this *new* covenant he made with us. I don't know about you, but when I consider marriage from this perspective, it makes the hairs on the back of my neck stand up in holy awe.

The Why Behind the Wait

So what does this have to do with marriage and sexuality? The answer: *Everything*. Marriage is more than a legal contract, a piece of paper, a ceremonial "I do," or a lavish wedding. It is an irrevocable covenant and is never to be entered into lightly. If we consider what we just explored, we can see that marriage covenant is to be a snapshot of the unending, everlasting relationship God longs to have with all humanity since the first seed sprouted in the Garden. The forever-ness of marriage is reflected in our physiology and why Jesus says in Mark 10:9 "Therefore, what God has joined together, no person is to separate" (NIV).

You don't have to squint your eyes to see that even in the secular world, marriage still follows covenantal tradition, whether we're conscious of it or not:

We no longer exchange physical coats, but we join *bank accounts* (for richer, for poorer!)

Warfare is not our everyday reality and we do not exchange weapons, although certainly vow to *protect* one another.

We exchange names. This is beginning to die out in the name of secular feminism, but traditionally the woman will take the last name of the man, inserting his name into hers. It's not an issue of gender inequality, it's an of issue covenantal procedure. A change of name signifies a change of life and identity, dawning from the enjoining of two old lives to become one new life.

Splitting of an actual animal would probably dampen the vibe at a wedding ceremony nowadays, but the meaning remains: "I will die before I'm unfaithful" or in familiar terminology *"Till death do us part!"*

The *promises* of the covenant are declared or literally "vowed" (if you hadn't guessed, that's what our 'vows' are) and the declaration of the oath is signed on a wedding certificate. Romantic movies in recent years tend to depict the vows as a collection of affirming words of the other person. But actually, the vows are meant to be a declaration of what the covenant entails: "In sickness and in health, for richer or for poorer, I will remain faithful to you."

The *sign* of covenant is demonstrated by the wedding rings. How do we know if someone is off the market? Just check for a ring on their left hand – it signifies to the world publicly that this couple are bound together in a special exclusive relationship.

Covenant witnesses are established. It is traditionally the maid of honour and the best man who witness and sign the wedding certificate. Even if you elope you still must have a witness to the ceremony, however informal, otherwise the marriage is not recognised by the government. For many it is an empty tradition, but the role of the witness is supposed to be to watch over the marriage covenant and speak up (like an angry Old Testament prophet!) if one party is unfaithful to the other.

The covenant meal is why weddings are followed by a feast or what we call a "wedding reception" where the community receives with joy the newly wedded couple for the first time. A new identity is always outworked in community, which is why our closest family and friends are invited to the reception.

Bloodshed ... Hold up, I don't remember any blood being shed at the weddings I've recently attended. Actually, this references when a woman loses her virginity and her hymen breaks. The woman is the creature born with the hymen, which means when the bride and groom consummate their relationship in marriage, there is usually a shedding of blood.

Blood is Thicker than Water

Genesis 2:24 describes the marriage covenant well, saying, "... a man leaves his father and mother and is united to his wife, and they become one flesh" (NIV). In this case, blood really is thicker than water: The blood of the covenant is thicker than the water of the womb from whence we come. Even if we might start blushing, the Jews of antiquity weren't awkward about this at all. In fact, they would consummate the marriage right there at the wedding! For them, sex was such a central part of married life and nothing to be ashamed about. Private and exclusive, but absolutely celebrated. (Remember, the pen of a Hebrew man wrote Song of Songs!)

At a Jewish wedding, the bridal chamber was located in the centre of the week-long celebration, and once the deed was done, the groomsman would stand outside the bridal chamber and wave the blood-stained sheets to the rest of the wedding party! Everyone would clap and cheer that the covenant had been consummated, sealed with blood, and any children born thereafter would be born *under the blood of the covenant,* therefore inheriting all the blessings of those promises made at the altar. In fact, it was the father who escorted his daughter to the bridal chamber and her parents kept the bloodstained bed sheet to prove their daughter's virginity at marriage – talk about a family affair![16] This illustration of covenant is both radically gracious and radically graphic. Whether it makes us sing or squirm, the picture is clear: We do not become "one flesh" from a de facto relationship, from love letters, or from being boyfriend and girlfriend. Two can only truly become one flesh through covenant, where two parties vow to commit their entire lives to one another. Blood simultaneously represents life and death, and this symbolises the idea of marriage: *Life* together, till *death* do us part. Sexual intimacy is the physical expression of this covenant oneness. It is the outward expression of the spiritual condition and *this* is why it is a spiritual experience as much as physical and emotional. Our biology and theology clasp hands to image our Eternal Creator: Humanity was created to be in covenant with God!

Virginity vs Purity

Although church culture continues to promote abstinence until marriage, there has been an interesting turn of the tide in secular Western culture when it comes to virginity. To lose your virginity prior to marriage was once considered a tragedy, and it still is today for some tribal communities in which covenant is entrenched in the culture. Today, being a virgin has become a reason to be taunted, mocked, and socially ostracised in the high school corridors of the West. But if we can be honest for a moment, it is not virginity that God has called us to, it's purity. Virginity and purity are not actually the same thing, despite the way Western Christianity has conflated the two, spawning what many are criticising as the *"toxic purity culture."* This derogatory label is used to describe the promoting of abstinence and sexual purity in church culture which appears to have mutated into a self-righteous and judgmental culture driven by pressure to conform to a standard of behaviour. Thereby, it inherited the term "toxic" for those who have fallen short. My guess is this has occurred because, once again, we have reduced virginity to a physical condition instead of connecting it to the heart. Somewhere along the way we began to treat it like a status to be lost instead of a gift to be given. Virginity should be esteemed, but not worn as a holier-than-thou badge of smugness.

Let's remember that virginity is not the *same* as purity; it should be the *fruit* of purity. It is possible to be a virgin with an impure heart. It is also possible for someone who gave away their virginity to make a Christ-led decision to repent and walk in sexual integrity once again. This is a gospel of the heart, which in turn affects our behaviour – not the other way around.

White Wedding Dresses

It is true that marriage is more about the life that follows the wedding than the wedding day itself. However, we can see how even the modern wedding ceremony is infused with covenantal symbolism. These days smaller, subdued weddings are on the rise as some turn a cynical eye upon the pageantry and lavish expenses of the multi-million dollar bridal industry. But tradition and symbolism are at the heart of the Christian faith, using physical and visual cues to prompt remembrance and faith in an unseen reality. The wedding dress, for example, is traditionally white because it is meant to symbolise the virginal purity of the bride.[17] For orthodox Jews, the bride's white dress symbolises that she has been ritually purified in preparation for her wedding, as does the groom's "kittel" (white linen coat).[18] The Apostle Paul plays on the metaphor of bridal purity when he writes of what Christ has done with *his* Bride, the Church, through the gospel: "He did this to present her to himself as a glorious church without a spot or wrinkle or any other blemish. Instead, she will be holy and without fault" (Eph 5:27).

Even in the West the wedding dress remains for most an important part of the ceremony. Expenses are poured out for the perfect style and fit. Some are custom designed, some use lace or tule or the finest materials. Brides-to-be pore over wedding magazines to find the "perfect dress." Hollywood has even jumped on board and made reality shows out of the experience. Why all the pomp and grandeur? Whatever culture we come from, the reason we don't wear a pair of ragged jeans as we walk down the aisle is because the dress is infused with meaning. It matters only because the covenant matters.

My wedding dress is custom made, with one-of-a-kind lace, cut and sewn to fit me perfectly. It was (and is) absolutely stunning and cost my mother more than I wish to say here. It now has mud stains around the bottom of the dress, which I actually love because it reminds me of the awesome fun I had at the wedding party. At the reception there was much joy, dancing, and singing, and the mud stains were an inevitable result of happy revelling. But if I had got that mud on my wedding dress *before* the ceremony it would have been a different story! I'm not sure there is a bride who exists who wants to walk down the aisle with a mud-stained dress, tomato sauce running down the front, messy hair, make up smudges or bad breath. There's something within us that wants to be spotless, pure, and untouched as we present ourselves before all our family and before our groom. We want to present ourselves in all our glory to him and have him echo Solomon's words, "You are altogether beautiful, my darling, beautiful in every way"

(Song of Sol 4:7). For this reason, we treat our wedding dress with care. It usually goes in a special bag before and after the *one* day it is worn. The bride-to-be hangs it in her wardrobe until the day comes and her bridesmaids help zip her into it. She's careful and vigilant with it, and for this reason, she doesn't wear it before the wedding day. She doesn't "practice" in her dress by wearing it out a few weekends beforehand. Nor does she do everyday errands in it, like working, shopping, cooking or exercising.

We don't treat a wedding dress like an everyday garment because it's *not* an everyday garment. We guard it from getting stained, trampled or torn, because we're saving it for something special – the day it was sewn together for. It's interesting that such elaborate care is still taken to attain and protect the wedding dress, but not so much the purity it is supposed to represent. There is a winsome beauty in purity, and the bridal industry makes a huge profit off this deeply ingrained desire of our hearts. Perhaps it's time to turn the dress inside out and remember the heart of the issue. For anyone who muddied their dress before the big day, rest assured, Christ can take it to the dry cleaners. The Scripture proves it.

David's Purity Restored

If you thumb the pages of Israel's history, some of their greatest leaders carried the greatest brokenness, particularly in the area of relationships and sexuality. Enter King David, Israel's most beloved king. The Bible famously repeats that *"he had a heart after God"* like an affectionate anthem. Jesus himself emerged from the blood line of David, so as an indispensable figure in history, we naturally want his relational track record to be squeaky clean. But most of the psalms we journal today are written from the aching corners of his heart, at times due to the repercussions of his own sin. David was a good king and a true worshipper but he was no stranger to sexual brokenness. He reaped some awful ramifications for it, and we have the opportunity to learn from, rather than repeat, the poison in his past.

The opening chapters of David and Bathsheba's infamous relationship are messy and painful, resembling more of a melodramatic soap opera than real life. But don't let the drama fool you into forgetting that these biblical characters were people with real, throbbing hearts. When laziness and luxury seduced David away from fighting for the kingdom, his eyes wandered over to Bathsheba's bath time. You probably know how the rest of the story goes. He took a woman who belonged to someone else and crossed about every boundary in the book to get her. David couldn't see the catastrophe of his sin until a prophet (a covenant witness) revealed it to him. Once David received a revelation of God's Word, his eyes were opened to just how disastrous his lustful affair was. As a result, he experienced the death of a child born from that ancient fling.

Now, remember, David was in a different covenant with God than you and I, and so different ramifications followed suit (which were heartbreaking to both David and the Lord). Forgiveness always follows repentance, but it doesn't always necessarily shield us from consequence. Just like David, we sometimes experience the fallout of our sin regardless of how much we try to pray it away.

David was no icon for virginity, but he became a beacon for purity – and whatever our past, so, too, can we. Yes, he endured grief and pain because of his sin. But God, in his infinite mercy and grace, gave him another promise. Another baby, and another chance to fulfil his calling by securing the royal bloodline. Solomon was born to David, and he ruled after him, keeping his family on the throne. Solomon, this *new* promise, grew to rule Israel's greatest period in history.

"Another chance" is the catch cry at the very heart of our gospel, and God has been chanting it since Genesis 3. And because of it, any person can sing the song of David's personal repentance while he's nursing the grave results of his own sexual sin: "Create in me a pure heart, oh God, and renew a right spirit within me" (Psalm 51:10). No self-help book, podcast or promise ring is going to help us here. It is the power of the Spirit of God alone that restores our purity.

Romans 3:24–26 (MSG) puts it as clear as mud: "Since we've compiled this long and sorry record as sinners (both us and them) and proved that we are utterly incapable of living the glorious lives God wills for us, God did it for us. Out of sheer generosity he put us in right standing with himself. A pure gift. He got us out of the mess we're in and restored us to where he always wanted us to be. And he did it by means of Jesus Christ."

Scripture testifies that purity can be restored and walked out no matter what our past has been like. Remember, marriage covenant is supposed to be a lived parable telling the story of the greatest covenant of all: the one Jesus made on behalf of all humanity. His shed blood cut a covenant of grace, and when our bank accounts join with his, we get to delve into the riches of his glorious forgiveness and restoration. We receive a pure heart that leads to clean hands. Our whole story, according to the Bible, will end in a huge wedding feast called "the Marriage Supper of the Lamb" (Revelation 19:6–9). You and I are invited, and he's already bleached our muddy outfits.

Before I met my husband, I'd spent my teenage years gambling a toxic relationship at Babel's Table and emerged broken and bruised. Thankfully, my broken heart lead me to my knees where I decided to take following Jesus seriously. To my surprise, he met me in such a radical way that my whole life was transformed. As I fell in love with my Saviour, my whole perspective on relationships and romance was reshaped by the life-giving words of Scripture. I regretted kissing a frog or two in my youth, but when I repented before God, I heard that gracious anthem: *another chance.* I wasn't really interested in romance for the time being, but rather was completely captivated by Jesus. He was and is the most enigmatic and enthralling person I've ever met, and no human person could compare. Nonetheless, I made the firm decision that when the time came to date someone, I was going to do it God's way. And just like David, God gave me another promise. Eventually I met the godly, passionate, wise man who is now my husband, and the rest is history. The long-anticipated moment where we faced one another at our wedding altar, my husband and I shared our very first kiss! We both joyfully bear witness to the fact that Christ not only forgives our past, but goes above and beyond to redeem and restore us. If we surrender our whole lives to him in obedience, He is faithful to bring us to wholeness and make us trophies of authentic purity.

"Blessed are the pure in heart, for they will see God" (Matt 5:8 NIV). We might not have our virginity, but we can have our purity. Whether we're stumbling onto the path of purity for the first time or we're considering whether it's even worth keeping on it, let me say this: at any point in time, you can make the choice to walk in sexual purity and wait for marriage in integrity. You're worth waiting for, friend. And the person you're going to spend the rest of your life with, well, they're worth waiting for too.

Men and Women in the Image of God

We've been reflecting on the biblical worldview of sex and marriage. If we're going to move onto dating, it's appropriate that we first consider what God says about men and women, especially in regard to how we interact with one another. As Bible-believing people, we draw our blueprints for male and female distinctions and relations from the creation narrative in Genesis 1 and 2. The testimony of Scripture declares that although men and women are *equal,* there is glorious beauty within their differences. We do ourselves no favours if we attempt to cover up our God-ordained distinctions with fig leaves, as Adam and Eve did in Gen 3:7! These differences are primarily determined by something extraordinary called D.N.A.

To help explain what this means, I want you to consider the book you're reading. This book is a compilation of words, and words are put together in a certain way to form what we call *language*. Language, of course, is the system of communication by which words are delivered. However, language only carries meaning because the words demand a speaker. Without a speaker, there is no language. Without an author, there are no words.

The Language of Life

Did you know D.N.A. is the most sophisticated language in the world? It is the very blueprint and language of life. It is by far the densest information storage mechanism in the world. In fact, one pinhead of D.N.A. is the equivalent to a pile of books reaching five hundred times the distance from here to the moon![1] And every single living thing is created from this code of life: D.N.A. So if language requires a speaker, than who is the Speaker of this highly advanced language? Avid evolutionists argue that D.N.A. is a product of *chance*, but still have to consent that it is a statistically improbable and mind-bending chance. The probability of the accidental formation of even one functional cell is acknowledged to be worse than 1 in 10^{57800}. (To give you some perspective, it would take 11 full pages of magazine type to print this number!)[2]

However, Christians know humans are no accident of atoms or chemical explosion. We dig no further than three verses into our Bible before we discover the answer. The very first recorded action we have is the Speaker speaking the language of life. Genesis 1:3 "Then God said ..."

The living God chose to use *words* to create life. This is why faith in God is far more appealing to many information scientists and computer scientists. The idea that all this vast and highly sophisticated information arose by dumb luck is ... well, dumb. The creation of life comes from D.N.A, the language of life. And only a *person* speaks with words or a language.

Boundaries are Blessed

If D.N.A. is the language that creates life, Genesis 1 records a stunning debut as we witness language pour straight from the mouth of God. Over and over in the creation narrative God speaks everything into being. Intriguingly, much of this is involving two related things:

Genesis 1:1 heavens *and* the earth
Genesis 1:3 light *and* darkness
Genesis 1:6 sky *and* water
Genesis 1:9 land *and* seas
Genesis 1:11 plants *and* trees
Genesis 1:14 sun *and* moon
Genesis 1:20 sea creatures *and* sky creatures
Genesis 1:24–26 land creatures *and* humans
Genesis 1:27 male *and* female

Right from the outset, the Bible presents these pairs as beautiful and blessed. When God was meticulously ordering and separating out creation into their categories, He was bringing order and design out of chaos and confusion. Genesis 1:2 tells us "... Now the earth was *formless and void*, and darkness was over the surface of the deep. And the Spirit of God was hovering over the surface of the waters" (emphasis mine).

That Hebrew word for *void* is "bo-hu" (וּבֹהוּ) meaning *total chaos, lack of order*.[3] When we reject the boundaries and definition God gave us in order to self-define and self-rule, chaos is inevitably what we return to. We'll learn in the next chapter that boundaries from God are always meant to bring freedom, not restriction.

With this is mind, I invite you to turn with me from chapter 1 of Genesis to chapter 2. Genesis 2 retells the same creation narrative, this time focusing intently on the two humans. God creates the *adam*, a word meaning *human*. Not a humanoid or primate, subject to fate, but a *human*. A curious being with eternity set in his heart, intrinsically marked and entirely set apart from the land, plants and animals. What makes the human distinct? The rest of creation is made "after their kind" but only humankind is specifically created in the *image* of God. This is why Christians do not believe we are like animals driven by biological urges, instinctively responding to our environment. We are volitional and moral beings that rule and reign *over* our environment. We are made in God's image, and thus He bestowed upon us a power and authority that the plants, animals, and planets to this very day did not receive. We are not enslaved to our environment but given the power to change it.

So Adam is placed in a garden where God puts him to sleep. While under holy anaesthesia, God creates another person from his rib, instead of the earth. Fortunately for Adam, science has now discovered that the rib is the one bone in the human body that can readily grow back![4] How curious that Eve is not made from the soil. Instead, she is made from flesh. Or to borrow Adam's poetic proclamation: *flesh of his flesh, bone of his bone!* (Gen 2:23) Eve is not made from lesser material than Adam, she is made from the *same* material. Just so you know, the biblical ideal of equality begins here, not with the secular feminists! Humanity is now complete because the human has a counterpart; side by side and heart to heart. As we have read in the previous chapters, it's not until this moment in Scripture that the text uses a different Hebrew word for Adam. The word *adam* meaning "human" changes to *ish* meaning "male." The Hebrew word for Eve is *isha* meaning "female." You might notice that his name is inserted into hers: *"isha"* contains the word *"ish"* which reflects their same root origin, but noting the distinction. Even in the English language, the word "woman" has the word "man" inserted within it, reflecting our sameness, but establishing the difference. We are inseparably linked, made from the same origins, but somehow distinguished from one another. The most immediate way Adam can tell is by looking at her genitalia. Since our body is intrinsically connected to our soul and spirit, our body plays a part in preaching the truth about who we are. She is the same, but gloriously *different!*

Male and Female He Created Them

The Bible records that from one human God made two humans: a male and a female. We can trace the first pair all the way back to Adam and Eve. The he has a she, and now the story of humanity can be marvellously complete. King and queen, ordained by God rule over every other living thing. Everything is meticulously organised after their own kind. Not a drop of creation is out of order. The Bible testifies that God is the only One who can do this special kind of work, and He views His work as *very good,* which in the Hebrew means "to the highest completive degree."[5] God's work isn't random or unplanned, arising from an atomic explosion or chaotic commotion. No, it's perfectly created so everything fits together and has the capacity to be fruitful. This includes the pinnacle of all God's creation, the male and the female, and explains why our bodies sexually fit together physically, like lock and key. Therefore, Christians believe that being made male or female is a *special work* that God owns the creative rights to. God's beautiful creation is not determined or altered by culture, trends, religion or ourselves. It is a truth preached by the language of D.N.A. – the language of life! His truth is something that is genetically written into our being where God's plans in eternity converge with our mother's womb.

God deliberately created man and woman with special distinctions so that when they united together, they'd have the capacity to be fruitful. In regard to sexuality, their bodily union has the capacity to beget more humans made in their image. By this means the earth can be filled with people to carry out God's good purposes and develop his creation.

Let's begin with the most obvious features. Men and women are *physically* different. Their body parts testify to 3 things:

1. They are the same
2. They are distinct
3. Together they bear the image of God

Genesis 2:15 tells us the man is placed in a garden to work it and cultivate it. Every seed Adam plants contains D.N.A., which you'll remember, is the building block of life. The soil, in this sense, is like a horticultural womb that receives the seed of D.N.A. and carries the potential to create life. Horticulturists are continually awed by this process, whereby the seed is genetically programmed to produce fruitfulness if the environment of the soil is diligently nurtured. But this is nothing compared to the human seed ...

The woman, however, is given an *internal* womb. She will receive the seed of D.N.A. from the man. In fact, the Greek word for "seed" is *sperma* and I'm sure you can guess the

English word we draw from that! Why? Because the male sperm carries D.N.A. It is united with the egg's D.N.A. and produces brand new, completely unique, never-before-seen, never-seen-again life in her womb. If Adam thought the new life born from the seeds he sowed in the garden was amazing, wait until he sees what will be yielded from Eve's womb!

We must be careful when we honour the sacred gender distinctions that we look at what Scripture *does* say, as opposed to what it doesn't. It does say that the male and female are different, having capacities that are the same, but also capacities that are distinct. For example, since the woman is the one to fall pregnant, the word *womb* is integrated into her name (woman). However, what Genesis is *not* saying is that, because men were not given the capacity to give birth, they cannot nurture and parent affectionately, tenderly and intimately. We are all created for intimacy and emotion, but must acknowledge that the way it is both expressed and generated differs between men and women. We've learned in chapter 3 how God has designed *both* men and women to release hormones to help them bond with their children and with one another, but while women release more oxytocin, men release more vasopressin. This is both interesting and mysterious. It seems these hormones bring us to the same end (bonding and intimacy) but the means by which it comes about differs for males and females.

Since Eve is the one given the womb, does that mean tilling the soil is Adam's domain alone? No, the intent of the author of Genesis is not to restrict the female gender from horticultural activities! Among many things, Genesis is revealing the blueprints for humanity, and in doing so, divulges truth about physiological differences. Men will never get physically pregnant, and generally speaking, women will never be physically as strong as men. This of course does not mean that women cannot be physically strong. However, by and large, the male gender will always be the physically stronger gender. You might come across a couple where the man is physically weaker and the woman is larger and stronger, but this is the exception to the rule when we study gender physiology. In high school I played football with the boys and could overpower several of them! But I was the exception to the rule, and I wouldn't want to prove that exception by trying out my strength on the professional football field. The reason we have to segregate most sports to make it fair is because, in general, men are stronger. They are biologically designed with more testosterone, and thus increased muscle mass, which is why it generally isn't fair to put men and women in the same categories for certain sports. To put it simply, men are the physically stronger vessel. It is for this reason that women are tragically subject to more violence, trafficking and subjugation on the planet then men.

This is exactly what Paul means when he writes about women being the *weaker* vessel. 1 Peter 3:7 "In the same way, you husbands must give honor to your wives. Treat your wife with understanding as you live together. She may be weaker than you are, but she is your equal partner in God's gift of new life …"

Many feminists don't like this word, but actually, Paul doesn't mean spiritually or ministerially weaker. He is simply stating the facts, that even a small child would be able to point out. The translation of the ancient Greek is the word *"ashenes"* (ἀσθενής) meaning physically weaker.[6] While it was common in Roman antiquity to violently exploit and dishonour women, Paul the Apostle writes in a remedial and protective sense, bestowing the honour and care upon women that radically countered his own culture, as well as our own. The BSB uses the best translation of the Greek to convey Paul's meaning: "Husbands, in the same way, treat your wives with consideration as a delicate vessel …"

Same But Different

What does "delicate" mean? By English definition it literally means *"very fine in texture or structure; of intricate workmanship or quality."* Physiologically, women are "finer" than men. Female skin is softer, while men have tougher skin. The female body is softer, since we have less genetic capacity for muscle. Although women of course can be muscular and athletic, soft fat sits on the chest, thighs, and hips more so than men. Men have physically larger brains, however, male and female brains have the same amount of neurones, meaning they have equal capacity for intelligence.

We might illustrate this by putting a mug and a fine china

teacup next to one another. Both are vessels that by and large do the same thing: they hold liquid so we can drink from them. They are completely equal in their potential. They are equal in their capacity. They can hold the same amount of boiling hot water and withstand the same amount of heat. They both have handles to grasp and rounded edges, meaning they are used in the same way. Despite their sameness, they're *different* in shape, texture and craftsmanship. A mug can be bought from the store, and you don't mind giving it to the toddlers because it can be knocked around a bit. Sure, it might get a chip or two, but it's sturdy and robust and can withstand a bit of rough manhandling (no pun intended!) The fine china teacup, on the other hand, is delicate. It's refined and admired in a different way. So what does Grandma do with her fine china? She puts it high up in a special place called the china cabinet. The china cabinet puts these special teacups on display, so everyone can witness their fine craftsmanship. Because the fine china is more delicate, it gets elevated to a place of special protection, so immature or rough people can't handle it in a way that breaks it.

By no means am I defining women by external beauty (though we can easily accuse Hollywood of relentlessly committing this offence). However, it is both a universal observation and a Scriptural principle that there is a winsomeness in women that men do not have. Babel culture attempts to either exploit it, reducing women to sexual objects rather than sacred image-bearers – or else strip it away entirely, exhorting women to forfeit or filter those traits and virtues that express their winsome femininity. For the countless women who don't view themselves as beautiful or winsome, perhaps it's because they've defined "beauty" by Babel, instead of the Bible. In a way, it is not difficult to wonder why vulnerable people find it difficult to embrace and celebrate their God-given body, since society in many ways degrades and distorts what was meant to be cherished and honoured.

Over and against Babel culture, Scripture presents a stunning reciprocity between men and women that is perhaps most wonderful to witness in the context of marriage and family. While it would be disappointingly inappropriate to reduce the role of women to child-bearing, it would be equally negligent to bypass the fact that women are endowed with a special capacity to carry very precious cargo. There is something heart-warming about watching a husband help and serve his heavily pregnant wife as she winces and waddles her way through the third trimester. She has been given a special strength to host, carry and deliver brand new life into the world. And while she is given this unique capacity, it is wonderful to watch the husband use his unique strength to carry and support her. He is able to carry and support the one who carries and supports the precious new life – and that new life is going to require *both* their strength, stewardship and unique input!

The creation narrative testifies that men and women both have value, dignity, potential and authority – but there is a preciousness to women that requires protecting. God has instilled something in every male (with a bit of help from vasopressin and testosterone) to shield that quality from being harmed. When bombs explode and bullets are flying, there is something valiant, chivalrous and protective within men that would (or should) rather go to the front line. In a world full of violent and frivolous men who, across many cultures and generations, have oppressed and violated women, Scripture charges husbands with an astonishing obligation to "...love your wives, just as Christ loved the church. He gave up his life for her" (Eph 5:25).

What Does Helper Mean?

We must never confuse the word "precious" for "flimsy." The description of being precious does not convey someone who lacks power. If this were so, perhaps God would have been better off choosing the male gender to travail in childbirth! God pours his power into every willing vessel, whether that be a mug or a teacup. Acts 2:17 proclaims "I will pour out my Spirit upon all people. Your sons and daughters will prophesy." Indeed, if we return to the creation narrative, God Himself describes Eve as a "helper" for Adam. This word has often been misinterpreted to imply that the one doing the helping is inferior to the one receiving help. This is an illogical interpretation, since we would never think of a teacher "helping" a student as inferior, nor of a parent "helping" their child! The Hebrew used to describe the woman is *"ezer kenegdo"* and the better English translation is "help-meet." This name is appropriately powerful, assigned to God Himself when He rescues His people. Out of the nineteen times it is found in the Old Testament, sixteen times it is used to reference "God our Helper" and the other 3 are used in reference to a military ally – but never once used as a subordinate.[7] It is notable that Jesus calls the Holy Spirit "The Helper" in the New Testament (Jn 14:26) who is in no way subservient within the godhead. Here in the creation narrative, Eve the helper is neither superior nor inferior to Adam, but equal. She is not superior in the way she helps, as though Adam were a helpless child depending on his mother. Neither is she an inferior brought along to be of some use to Adam in the garden or exclusively for procreational purposes. And though women may be precious, they are no less powerful than men. Perhaps the confusion and power-struggles that fill our debate panels and media feeds would be appeased if we acknowledged that *both* genders are powerful, yet the way in which that power is administrated is different. Women are allowed to be mighty yet delicate. Men are allowed to be robust yet tender. We are exhorted by Scripture to use the unique strengths pertaining to our gender to serve and uphold one another, not pin each other down in order to control or belittle the opposite sex.

Paul the Apostle affirms this paradox of delicate strength when he sends greetings to the sisters, Tryphena and Tryphosa, in this letter to the Roman church (Rom 16:12). He explicitly commends them for being women who "work hard in the Lord." This is very likely a play on words, since their names meant "delicate" (Tryphena) and "dainty" (Tryphosa).[8] Paul emphasises that despite their outward daintiness, these women were mighty labourers for the gospel and God was powerfully at work through them. The gospel declares that the same Spirit that lives within Christian men is the same Spirit that lives within Christian women. The Spirit is not somehow diluted or weakened when He resides in the "delicate" female vessel. The work of the Holy Spirit in and through us bestows dignity upon both genders, right down to every pinhead of D.N.A. To repeat with the summations we began with: men and women are the same, yet we are distinct, and together we bear the image of God!

Emotional and Sexual Differences

Many have chuckled over the differences between men and women, lamenting that at times it seems as if we come from different planets. This becomes even more obvious when we enter the bedroom! It's no secret that men and women tend to feel and think differently when it comes to sex, and this of course inevitably effects how we feel and think about dating. Men tend to be more visually wired when it comes to sex, responding to visual stimuli and having a typically higher sex-drive in part due to higher levels of testosterone. This is why, for example, a much higher percentage of males get hooked on pornography than females. Women, on the other hand, tend to be more emotionally wired, responding to emotional stimuli, in part due to having a larger limbic system and higher levels of oestrogen. This is why a higher percentage of women find it more difficult than men to get over a breakup, especially if the couple has engaged sexually. Usually she has connected emotionally to the sexual activity in a stronger way than him.

Because of her emotional wiring, a woman tends to open up to *sexual* intimacy if she feels *emotional* intimacy first. She needs to feel loved, adored and cherished through things like meaningful conversation, acts of care and service, and unconditional (non-sexual) affection. Because he is wired visually, a man tends to open up to *emotional* intimacy much more deeply through means of *sexual* intimacy. Men do want emotional intimacy and closeness, but tend to approach it and express it through sexual intimacy.[9]

To make it even more complex, men tend to release their stress through sex. All those wonderful hormones and endorphins become a great antidote to his anxiety and frustration. And so the more stressed he is, the more he desires to release this stress through sexual means. Unfortunately for him, stress tends to have the opposite affect on women. The more pent-up stress and anxiety she has, the less she tends to want to engage in sex with her partner.

Because of these differences, sometimes women are portrayed in movies as overly needy, emotion-leeches who have little sexual desire. It's a shallow caricature that misunderstands the way she actually ticks. At the same time, men can be likewise unfairly stereotyped as insensitive users who are only interested in sex, with little emotional capacity or care. But these differences are not ruling out the fact that men have emotional needs and women have sexual needs. It's just that a husband is more likely to get his sexual needs met if he meets her emotional needs. And a wife is more likely to have her emotional needs met if she meets his sexual needs. This means that we have to honour each other's differences and put our spouse before ourself. God has once again rigged the system so that the only way to unlock what we desire from one another is to *serve the other partner's needs first*. Both parties live out the sexual gospel by committing to "submit to one another out of reverence for Christ" (Eph 5:21). You can see how our different wiring sets us up for great vulnerability and even violation if we're with someone selfish and manipulative. Paul safeguards us against this with the words of Ephesians 5:25–29 "… In the same way, husbands ought to love their wives as they love their own bodies. For a man who loves his wife actually shows love for himself. No one hates his own body but feeds and cares for it, just as Christ cares for the church."

The man and woman must lay down their lives (their own needs and desires) in submission to one another in order to bless and serve one another other! When both covenant parties are committing to put each other first, embrace and celebrate each other's strengths, cover one another's vulnerabilities …

they will be fruitful and multiply in every way, and I'm not just talking about procreation. They will have a fruitful marriage, a fruitful family, a fruitful ministry, a fruitful calling – because we have fruitful origins! Humanity was born in a garden, and the gospel continually paves the way back.

Limitation vs Celebration

The differences between males and females are not for limitation, but celebration! We need not run for the fig leaves to cover over our differences. They are reason to *appreciate* one another, not control, manipulate or divide. As we have seen, men and women have certain characteristics, dispositions and attributes that are the same, yet others that are distinct. Personalities, spiritual gifts and various predispositions make this all even more dynamic. Why did God create us with such differences? Because as we acknowledge the *diversity* between men and women, yet come together in *unity*, we will fulfil the great commission of Genesis 1:27 to "be fruitful and multiply."

Diversity and unity is where we get the English word "university", which actually comes from the Latin word *universitas* meaning 'the whole'. When the male and female distinctions are honoured, in and out of the bedroom, we get the *whole* picture of fruitful and joyful relationships. This is by no means restricted to romantic relationships. The Church should stand in stark contrast to the conflict and confusion that plagues humanity. Kingdom sons and daughters are to celebrate one another, fostering powerful unity between men and women that is winsome to a watching world.

A scan of Facebook or Twitter reveals polarising and reactionary feelings whenever gender is the topic of the conversation, often aptly named "the battle of the sexes". Why do these subjects evoke such a feverish response from us? The reality is, it is deeply and innately connected to our identity. These conversations are about what makes us who we *are*, and we are rightfully impassioned about it. Since you are the common denominator in every relationship you will have, knowing who you are is foundational to having healthy relationships. The Word of God beautifully and unapologetically determines our identity. However, it's no surprise that there is much confusion around this issue as contemporary culture drifts from a biblical worldview. The Tower of Babel narrative tells us that God confused the *language* of the rebellious coalition of builders. To be sure, confusion around identity is not God's initiative, but the prevailing sermon Babel teaches us is that when we construct ideas devoid of God's truth, we will inevitably be thrust into confusion.

Identity in the Image of God

We are created to be known and named. Sexual intimacy is a wonderful way to know and be known by our spouse, but it cannot be our starting point. We must start by knowing and being known by our God, and it is the Bible that tells us who we are and Whose we are. It's no surprise that people are facing an identity crisis as a result of being taught that their origin story is an accident of atoms, instead of being purposefully made by a loving Creator who has a destiny for their life. If we don't know God, we don't know who we are. When we don't know who we are, we end up afraid, confused, and unhappy. As we reject the Bible's blueprints, we try to formulate our own identity and make our own rules. This is known as *expressive individualism*, which as we've discussed, is an aching symptom of our humanistic culture. It fills this vacuum of truth by presenting identity as something that is subjective and transitory. In simple terms: you can define who you are, and that definition can change. This fluctuation might be driven by our feelings, the community we surround ourselves with or ideology we subscribe to on any given day. But things like feelings, peers, opinions, and trending ideas are all subject to human failure and fracture. We need something more stable than that. Identity is something that needs to be unchanging and anchored in truth for us to flourish as humans. We need to know who we are even when we have a bad day, or our peers have rejected us, or we've failed miserably.

Our heartache reveals an innate desire within all of us: we are searching for a *name*. We want to be *known*. What is identity? Identity is the answer to the question "Who am I?" By dictionary definition, it is the fact of *being* who one *is*. Humanity won't find the answer to this existential question in the amount of social media followers they count, titles they use, filters they choose or fig leaves they fashion. A quick glance on social media reveals these frenzied attempts to ascribe to ourselves an identity. People are searching for descriptions and ways to express themselves that help communicate who they are, what makes them significant and where they fit in society. And who can blame them? The Religion of Social Media preaches a theology of specialness, where people are repeatedly exhorted to be exceptional by influencers on their digital pulpits. In order to achieve significance and distinction they must break outside the "norm." To be normal or, dare I say it, even *boring* would be the worst kind of damnation. But our specialness has nothing to do with what we call ourselves, and everything to do with whose image we are made in: God.

Our identity is rooted and discovered in the Garden of Eden, where God gave us the blueprints of loving origins, gender, community, authority and destiny. Genesis tells us this identity was distorted by sin in the garden (the Fall) and we've been trying to find it ever since. We desperately want to be known uniquely, personally and individually – and many don't realise that this inherent longing is only found in being known by the God who made us uniquely, personally and individually. He knows, as the Psalmist says, every hair on our head – or in modern terminology, every pinhead of D.N.A! Psalm 139:15–17 "You watched me as I was being formed in utter seclusion, as I was woven together in the dark of the womb. You saw me before I was born. Every day of my life was recorded in your book. Every moment was laid out before a single day had passed. How precious are your thoughts about me, O God. They cannot be numbered!"

Fig Leaves & Forgiveness

The first man and woman were made in covenant with God, and with each other, with Genesis 2:25 describing them as "naked and unashamed." We might read over this, but this is a profound declaration in an era where shame and sexuality are often found in the same sentence. Before the Fall, there was no self-hatred, no shame, no identity confusion, nor any hinderance to wholesome and fruitful intimacy. Genesis 3:7 tells us that when the first humans disobeyed God and ate the forbidden fruit "At that moment their eyes were opened, and they suddenly felt shame at their nakedness. So they sewed fig leaves together to cover themselves." Shame can drive us to do some unimaginable and, to be honest, completely irrational things. I'm not sure why Adam and Eve thought the trees would suffice as a hiding spot from an omnipresent God. It was shame that compelled them to hide their private parts with fig leaves, in a feeble attempt to cover for themselves. What is significant for us, is that this shame was directed towards their differences: they covered their genitalia.

If you follow the creation narrative closely, you'll notice that God sacrificed an animal (Gen 3:21) in order to make clothing for Adam and Eve. Do not make light of this verse. It is heavy with Gospel glory. The blood of the first animal slain was to atone for the sin of the first male and female. Death must precede life. Judgement must precede grace. This animal was judged for the sin of Adam and Eve. In an unforeseen act of mercy, God used the skin of the unnamed animal to clothe them, and hide their shame. He brought them out of hiding, and instead hid their shame behind the skin of the innocent, who bled and died for them. It becomes the foundation of the entire sacrificial system of the Old Testament, where animal after animal endured sacrificial death to exonerate humans of judgement and shame. Until one day, God would not send an animal. He would send His Son.

Friends, Christ is the fulfilment of Genesis 3:21. He is the Innocent One, the Lamb slain, taking upon himself the judgement of the sinner. His sacrifice covers us: all our sin, our shame, our brokenness, our confusion, our sexual immorality, our skewed identity. It is now *hidden* in Christ, covered by the skin of the Lamb, nailed to his innocence. Adam and Eve refused to bow to God's command in the garden of Eden, so Christ kneeled in the garden of Gethsemane. Because of his final and historic sacrifice, what we lost in Eden is triumphantly rediscovered at the cross. This is what it means to be made into a "new creation" as Paul joyfully exclaims in 2 Corinthians 5:17. His words should remind us of the *first* creation. In other words, we get a do-over of the Garden of Eden. We get another shot at the creation narrative, except instead of writing it in Scripture we are writing it with our lives. We are given a new nature, and with it, a new name. This name is what will identify us and define who we are. What is this new identity? Friends, we are now called *Christians*.

Colossians 3:3 "For you died to this life, and your real life is hidden with Christ in God." What does this mean? It means everything you long for is discovered in him. It means in order to find out who you really are, you must find out who *he* is. You must abandon self-made fig leaves and all attempts to self-identify. For the confused, the questioning, the rejected and the broken, the gospel is not a message of transitory identity – but transformational identity. Indeed, Isaiah 62:2 tells us "And you will be called by a new name, Which the mouth of the Lord will designate."

Boundaries to Blessings

It's all very well to marvel at a beautiful garden and appreciate it... but it's an entirely other thing to put your hand to the plough and know how to get there. So, now that we have vision for wholesome sex, we can talk about how we can landscape it by way of healthy boundaries. So, what is a boundary? Many books have been written on this increasingly popular subject and I won't attempt to do the same. At their core, boundaries send a message: this is valuable, and it belongs to me.[1] They do this by separating and defining what they protect. A fence is a boundary that protects a garden, separating it from the neighbours' yard and defining it as the owner's. "No" is a verbal boundary that protects our consent, defining both our autonomy and personal desires. Biblical commands are moral boundaries, separating good from evil and defining morality. Naturally and spiritually speaking, boundaries are everywhere, and always have been. From the beginning,

"... God saw that the light was good. Then he separated the light from the darkness" (Gen 1:4). He gave his creation boundaries ... and that includes us!

Ancient Walls

One of the most noticeable boundaries in antiquity was *walls*. Jerusalem (and all ancient cities) had imposing walls surrounding them. Cities were usually built on a hill and from a distance the walls were the most obvious feature to be seen from afar. They were so substantial that they are often the most prominent remains excavated by archaeologists. They were also very expensive; a great amount of resources and energy were required to build a city's walls and the tax payers were well aware of it.[2] Why pay the price for such big boundaries? They were the very structure that stood between enemy assault and the civilians, and so provided peace and wellbeing for the people who lived inside. You can imagine the emotional and spiritual attachment the ancient people had to their walls. They even wrote *love* songs about their walls! (See Psalm 122)

It's the reason the books of Ezra and Nehemiah carry such great weight in the biblical story as they document the rebuilding of Israel's walls after they were destroyed in exile. Walls became a metaphor for salvation, not just physically from military enemies, but spiritually. Isaiah 60:18 exclaims "You shall call your walls salvation and your gates praise" (NIV).

To put it plainly, the boundaries around the city became blessings to the people within them. And it is no different to the boundaries we put in our own relationships.

Modern Walls

Walls around cities might be a thing of the past but boundaries abound in modernity. If you want to spot them, look for something really expensive. A keen observation will reveal that the higher the value of something the more effort exerted to protect it with boundaries. So when we really think about it, boundaries are not so much for restriction, but protection. It's not about trapping something (or someone!) *in*, it's about keeping harm *out*. It's about preserving something precious, whether it's people within city walls or sex within marriage.

We've all seen those spy movies where thieves try to steal the giant jewel in the centre of the museum. It's guarded by all manner of different restrictions: ropes, lasers, security cameras, security guards and of course the classic thick glass box it's encased in. Basically, nobody can get to the jewel because it's surrounded by boundaries! Boundaries that send a message: this is valuable, and only the privileged can touch it.

The privileged person who gets to handle the jewel is the person who can be *trusted* with it. The person we are 100% certain will not steal it and sell it for their own selfish gain. They will not damage it in their clumsiness or carelessness.

They won't misuse and abuse it. They're going to wear special cotton gloves so as not to smudge the jewel with the dirt and oils on their hands. Usually this person is the museum owner or an absolute professional who has undergone the process of proving they are trustworthy. They go through a series of interviews, training, and time, to ensure their trustworthiness with something so simultaneously precious and vulnerable.

Dating Defined

This is helpful when we attempt to define the modern concept of "dating." Defining something that is not in the Bible is no easy task, and after reading many Christian books on the subject to help pastor young people, I have found that drawing lines where the Bible doesn't quickly leads to legalism or rebellion. Dating is simply the modern label we use for the *process of proving you are trustworthy*. We can call it whatever we want. Last century people called it courting. Today some might call it dating. I might call it friendship with intentionality. Americans might call it something different to Australians. The label doesn't matter so much as the process.

The issue is that we want the person we marry to be someone who has *proven* that they are trustworthy to handle what is most precious and prized: our heart, mind and body. This takes time (experiencing life together), training (growing in maturity and learning how to steward someone's heart) and interviews (getting to know one another through observation and conversation).

We must undergo a process with people to prove that they are trustworthy. And by the way, you have to prove yourself trustworthy as well. You might be exposed through this 'process' that you're not quite up for the task either. If they have proven (like the museum owner) the trust, integrity and ability required to handle the prized gem, then we can give them access to it. But do not give people permission right up front – not everybody gets immediate access to the diamond. What makes a diamond valuable is that you don't find them in grocery stores, vending machines or on the street. They are not readily available for the flippant spender. We live in an all-access generation, where we define sexual freedom by our ability to give anyone we want an all-access pass to our bodies and hearts. It is interesting that we exert so much protection over objects of value like diamonds, gems and money, but not nearly so much with the pinnacle of all created things: ourselves. As we undergo this process of time, training and interviewing, we can slowly give increased access and filter out inappropriate people. The final proof of worthiness to handle the prized gem of sexuality is marriage. You can only trust someone with your entire self (body, mind, and heart) if they have laid down their lives for you. (We discussed this thoroughly in chapter 4.) In the meantime, we will put appropriate boundaries in place to protect something so precious yet so vulnerable.

We Protect What We Value

The issue of boundaries is one of self-worth. We will only *guard* ourselves to the degree that we *value* ourselves. Have you noticed that the people who don't value themselves tend to have very little boundaries? If you don't think yourself worthy of blessing, you won't put in the boundaries that lead to it. However, the truth is, no matter where you come from or what your history, gender or belief system is, you are still made in the image of God. Being an image-bearer is not a *Christian* thing, it's a *human* thing. Being created in the image of God ascribes you with honour, worth and dignity before you've even taken a breath outside of your mother's womb. But when a generation moves away from the very Bible that reminds us of this, an inevitable drop in self-esteem and self-worth will follow. We won't safeguard our heart if we don't realise its inherent value. We won't protect our bodies if we don't respect them. We won't put boundaries around sexuality if we don't regard it as something precious for a purpose. We won't lay down boundaries in our relationships if we don't value ourselves, or the other person. You get the idea.

The reason I have a lock on the front door of my house is because I value the people and possessions inside. For this same reason, not everybody gets access to my house. Unsafe people who come into my house uninvited are called intruders. Far from being innocent, intruders are people who violate my boundaries and values by breaking in and are likely to rob me. Many people are robbed in relationships because they lack sturdy relationship boundaries that lock out inappropriate people. Please do not confuse the word *inappropriate* with *unworthy*. When you have boundaries that do not allow someone past a certain point, it is not communicating to them that they are unworthy or invaluable. It's communicating that you *are*. Your heart and sexuality are precious, and you won't be giving them away for free.

Relationships lacking good boundaries give selfish people easy access. This is what we call being 'used' by someone, and a user is of course a selfish person, even if they come across friendly. They come in, take what they want, and they leave. Remember the walls around Jerusalem weren't for *restriction* to trap people in, they were for *protection* to keep intruders out. So let's think about building boundaries in our relationships the way God's people treasured their walls.

Garden Walls

Before we think this is a departure from our garden analogy, remember that gardens by their very nature have structure and boundaries. What separates a garden from wild flora? It's the order and structure. Eden was a sanctuary of order, life and design in a world previously consisting of chaos and darkness. Genesis 2:15 tells us that "The Lord God took the man and put him in the Garden of Eden to work it and take care of it" (NIV).

There is intentionality in a garden that stands in contrast to the wild, where everything grows everywhere without restraint. I remember when my husband planted beans in our garden before we left for a vacation. By the time we came home, the beans had gone wild! Because he hadn't put stakes in the garden, the rapidly growing beans had no structure to grow up and around. Without these boundaries, they grew in every direction in a tangled mess, smothering the other vegetables planted nearby. We learnt a valuable lesson about the need for boundaries in our garden that day!

In chapter 1 we discussed that our calling is to extend the Garden, representative of the Kingdom of God, through wholesome kingdom relationships. If this is so, than implementing boundaries very much apart of how we will steward and grow these relationships. Any gardener will tell you that structure within a garden is what helps keep it healthy and fruitful. Some seeds need to be placed a certain distance apart. Fast-growing plants (like the infamous beans) require stakes to grow around so they don't tangle and suffocate other plants. Pathways need to be created in the garden for the gardener to walk through and provide tending and care. Some plants need to be situated in shade while others require more sun.

These are all examples of boundaries, but the difference is that these boundaries are organic and flexible; subject to as much change as the seasonal plants themselves. Just as with the excitable beans, the stake doesn't control, suppress or restrict them. It serves them. It exists as a framework to direct their growth. If the stake could talk, it would say "You can lean on me." If boundaries in relationships could talk, they'd say the same thing! They simply provide the framework for the relationship to grow healthily, without bringing harmful entanglement (and suffocation) to any people involved. When we're overexcited (as we often are in romantically charged situations!) boundaries give us structure to fall back on and keep the relationship standing upright.

Boundaries within our relationships should be flexible, and subject to appropriate change as the relationship itself grows. And of course, every garden needs walls or fences to protect us from slithering intruders!

The difference between garden structure and Babel, is that Babel goes *up* and the garden goes *out* (as discussed in chapter 1). The Babel attitude implements scaffolding with the motivation to build for Self and ego. The Garden mindset implements structure to grow outward, not simply for the sake of self but protecting others. Babel's structure is permanent and immoveable, built with bricks and mortar that once laid, are laid for good. Garden structure is flexible and organic, able to be adjusted as the seasons inevitably change. So, now that we realise boundaries are to protect blessings, let's go ahead and build some garden walls into our relationships ...

Physical Boundaries

Physical boundaries are of course the most obvious boundary to implement when it comes to romance. We must install strong "stakes" into our physical and digital environments. If we're struggling with lust, than even more stakes need to be plunged into those relationships for our own protection, as well as others. Let's say you're on a special diet in order to get free from sickness. Hanging out in the kitchen and constantly staring at the fridge is not going to be helpful. Even worse, going to the local supermarket and perusing the confectionary isle is going to stir up an appetite in you that you are trying to break free from. In the same way, if you're goal is to be free from a lustful appetite, than certain places and spaces will need to be off-limits until your mind is transformed. This shouldn't make us indignant, since the Bible commands fasting from certain foods and activities in reverence to God. Abstaining from certain activities and places in order to achieve victory over lust is a worthwhile boundary to implement, even if temporary. Some boundaries, of course, are permanent. Digital environments are more difficult to avoid, since we live in an era where we carry the world in our back pocket. Firm boundaries must be put in place when it comes to what we view on our phones, especially when it comes to scrolling through sexual or morally ambiguous content. A screen does not separate us from sin. If I steal a million dollars through digital fraud, I won't be pardoned because I didn't physically grasp the money in my own hand. Viewing sexually immoral content through a screen does not exempt us from participating in the activity. If someone views a stripper online, according to Jesus (Matt 5:28) it's the same as being in the room.

People who struggle with viewing pornography are going to find it very difficult to break free if they don't know how to unhook from their phone. Long gone are the days where one could simply avoid the adult store and R rated movies to steer clear of perversion. Nowadays unlimited pornography can be accessed with ease (and in the privacy of people's homes) as broken people caress glass screens, feeding an increasingly powerful addiction. Even more unfortunate is that smartphones are addictive in and of themselves. Combining sexual perversion, such as porn, with an addictive device, such as a smartphone, is a recipe for a porn pandemic – one of the most insidious global diseases infecting us today. A phone addiction and porn addiction go hand in hand, and you cannot break one without breaking the other. We need to implement some serious quarantine restrictions in order to get free from lust.

Physical boundaries are of course not limited to sexual boundaries. The Bible tells us that crossing sexual boundaries prior to marriage is a sin that inevitably robs both parties of sexual blessing, but it's also helpful to remember that certain levels of touch are just a stone's throw away. Even a long hug triggers the trust-circuits in a female brain whether a man has earned her trust or not.[3] Yes, we must take care who we envelop in intimate hugs! It can convince our brain to trust someone who has not in reality earned that trust. Knowing where to draw the line is about setting you both up for success. Remember, we're meant to pray "lead me *not* into temptation" not lead *ourselves* into temptation!

Without fail, the number one question that is most frequently asked is "how far is too far?" when it comes to honouring boundaries with a romantic interest. However, if we're asking this question we're probably coming from the wrong angle. When we ask that question, what we're really asking is "how far can I go without sinning, but still gratify my desires?" We want to know where the line is so we can go as close to it as possible while safeguarding our sense of purity, but it's a self-oriented question. We should instead be asking the question "what completely and wholeheartedly honours and esteems this person? How can I protect this person's heart? How can I safeguard their body and soul?" This is an *others*-oriented question and much clearer to answer.

Until we're at the wedding altar, they're actually not ours. The reality of this means we could be interacting with someone else's future spouse. So rather than making rules to follow, let's ask the question "if they *did* marry someone else, could I look their future spouse in the eye and know that I stewarded that person's heart in a way that honours them?" That question becomes a lot easier to answer, since you don't really need to legislate love or honour. I don't need to give you a list of rules and draw lines in the sand to say "This far and no more. Keep yourself at least 10 inches apart at all times and no snuggling under the blankets together!" As we cultivate a relationship with the Holy Spirit and Scripture, He will convict us if we're dishonouring the other person or leading one another into temptation.

Social Boundaries

Just as mould grows in dark hidden spaces, boundaries are usually crossed when we are hidden from the sight of others. It's human nature to stumble when we don't have the accountability of other people's eyeballs! This is why God sets us in community and family. Quite simply, we need one another. When it comes to dating, hanging out in groups is a great way to build trust and free us from the pressure of getting to know someone in an exclusively romantic environment. There's nothing inherently *wrong* with a romantically charged environment, it's just that it makes our hormones go crazy. You know, those bonding ones we talked about in chapter 2.

Those bonding chemicals are also blinding chemicals! You've heard the phrase *"love is blind"* in love songs, rom-coms, and weaved affectionately into conversation. The statement may be corny, but it's actually somewhat true. When we're attracted to someone our brain releases neurochemicals that dilute the other person's faults and magnifies their good traits. The butterflies, the hormones, the emotions, the attraction – they intoxicate us, blurring our vision, making it difficult to make rational, objective decisions. It's actually something that happens to our brain called *focalism* which takes place in any situation filled with intense excitement, tension or emotion.[4] Focalism is where we focus on one infatuating thing whilst conveniently excluding all the other facts.

Since God designed us this way, it's not a bad thing, it's just a *risky* thing. It's a little like trying to drive while inebriated (which, to be clear, *is* a bad thing!) Our inhibitions are lowered, our perspective is blurred, and we can even put others in danger. In fact, we can become blind-drunk to the reality around us: *"He's cute. He said he loves me,"* so our brain conveniently ignores the fact that he's rude to his mother, disrespectful to other girls, and he doesn't share our faith. Hanging out in groups allows us to witness how a potential partner interacts with other people and it's great for friends to provide feedback as well. How someone treats others is a foretaste of how they'll one day treat their partner once that rose-colored focalism wears off.

Getting love-drunk might feel really good in the moment, but we can wake up with a relational hangover of pain and regret, especially if we hurt someone else on the road. So how do we drive safely? We need a designated driver, so to speak! We need community of parents, pastors, friends and leaders who can look at the relationship from a sober perspective. We need people to help us make good choices because when we're attracted to someone, no matter how wise we think we are, we will rarely make an objective decision. Dating in isolation robs us of the wisdom we need to navigate this enjoyable but intoxicating world of romance. Proverbs 27:6 might sting a little, but it could save us from some seriously creepy or toxic people: "Wounds from a sincere friend are better than many kisses from an enemy."

Yes, love is blind. But that impairment doesn't have to lead us into a car crash or relational disaster. God gave us the gift of choice, but He sent the Holy Spirit to guide, lead, and compel those choices in a way that leads to life and love. The Holy Spirit isn't the cop that pulls you over when you've broken the law, He's the friend that tells you when you're driving dangerously. Really, social boundaries are about surrounding yourself with people who champion purity and biblical sexuality. On the flip side of this, if your only social group is made up of friends who support worldly ideals and sexual immorality, then you're going to have to consider social boundaries in your friendships as well. Since God has fashioned us for community, we're highly influenced by those we spend time with, especially those we like.

When my husband got saved in his teens, he had to distance himself from some of his social group who frequently took drugs so that he himself could break free from the temptation and become the person God called him to be. It was a painful but necessary social boundary, and not one that he regrets in the slightest. He had to sacrifice approval and reputation with those people, but it was a sacrifice Jesus was worthy of. Years later, some of those people have expressed a desire to have the marriage and family he has. Reaching our unsaved friends for Christ is always a noble and appropriate desire, but we cannot transform the people in our world unless we ourselves are first transformed.

Mental Boundaries

As we have hopefully seen, boundaries are certainly not restricted to our actions. Paul the apostle wrote "let God transform you into a new person by changing the way you think" (Romans 12:2). So powerful is the mind that it is the centre of our transformation! If our thoughts have such power to change our lives, we'd better protect them. Rather than letting our feelings rule our thought life, we need to put boundaries around our thinking and essentially tell our thoughts where to go.

Song of Solomon is a book laced with garden imagery and 2:15 warns of keeping the foxes from infiltrating the vineyard. Foxes native to Palestine were silent and sly in nature, but destructive to vineyards due to their penchant for grapes. Like foxes, intrusive and unwelcome thoughts can slip silently into our mind and wreak havoc from the inside out. Repeated thoughts can dig out ravines through which attitudes, addictions, and mindsets flow.

For example, if we invest a lot of fantasy and imagination into someone we're interested in, we'll feel a mental void if the friendship ends. Or worse, we won't be able to stop thinking about them when they end up with someone else, because we've created an unhealthy mental attachment. Those who have meditated on someone obsessively find it very difficult to move on. This is probably a good time to caution us that we need to have boundaries around what kind of music we listen to, books we read and movies or shows we watch. For example, listening to the kind of music that sexualises and objectifies women is not going to produce a wholesome thought life. Watching movies that explicitly promote and normalise lust will also weave their way into our thoughts sooner or later. The reason our thoughts matter, is because lustful thoughts will lead to perverted actions, as Jesus taught in Matthew 5:27. In fact, any obsessive thought that isn't fixed on Christ is a form of false worship. For this reason, when we're navigating romantic relationships, Phil 4:8 is a powerful boundary: "Fix your thoughts on what is true, and honourable, and right, and pure, and lovely, and admirable. Think about things that are excellent and worthy of praise."

Spiritual Boundaries

What are the spiritual boundaries we should take into account when it comes to romance? 2 Corinthians 6:14 says "Do not be yoked together with unbelievers" (NIV). Paul is not speaking about marriage specifically here, but being yoked in spiritual worship with an unbeliever. Marriage and dating, of course, fit perfectly into this category, since we want the person we marry to worship the same God that we do! The idea is this: yoking ourselves romantically to someone who does not hold your same Christian virtues sets us up for strife.

Before we start bristling in defence, this is fair to both parties here. The phraseology of "yoke" comes from the law of Moses. In the Old Testament they weren't allowed to hitch two animals of different species together when they were ploughing. They were not to be 'unequally' yoked (Deut 22:1). For example, if you yoked a donkey and an ox together, they'd go different speeds and different directions.[5] Donkeys are designed to carry loads, and stubbornly dig their heels in when needed. Oxen are designed to pull a plough and they're trained to keep plodding along. You're setting both creatures up for strife and failure, which would be unfair to both of them.

The Bible says anyone in Christ is a new *creation* (2 Cor 5:12). This means that when we're saved we become a new creature and inherit a new *nature*. If you're a new creation, dating someone who isn't a Christian is like dating another species. They're actually in a different kingdom, and they have a different nature to you. It's unfair to them (as well as you) to hitch yourself to someone in another kingdom. Yoking our lives with someone who isn't a believer will usually lead to one of two things: we'll compromise and go in their direction or we'll impose behaviour modification (which is legalism) on them to conform to our standards. Neither option sets us up for spiritual peace and relational harmony.

It's important to note however, that Paul is not telling married Christians to divorce their unbelieving partners if they're *already* married. This is an entirely different subject. Mixed marriages weren't totally uncommon in the early Church because many Gentiles who were already married got saved, but their spouse remained unbelievers. To that Paul prescribes different advice: Honour your commitment and continue to witness to your spouse, having faith that God will save them too (1 Cor 7:10–16). In any case, marriage is not the subject of this chapter and the prevailing idea is this: Donkeys and oxen don't belong together, and when we're choosing our life partner it is wise to yoke ourselves to someone who has the same nature as us.

Being equally yoked with our partner is not just restricted to two believers. A racehorse and Clydesdale are technically both horses, but it would still be unwise to hitch them together since one goes really fast and one goes really slow. It's not impossible to make it work, but worthy to take into consideration before we decide to hitch our lives to someone. We do not necessarily need to share the same hobbies and taste in coffee, but our lives need to be orientating around the same value systems and headed in the same direction. Are we prepared for the sacrifice required to slow down if we naturally go fast? Are we willing to speed up for the sake of our spouse, if we're someone who likes to plod along in life? These are worthy questions to ask before deciding on a wedding venue and caterer!

Likewise, consideration should be taken when it comes to yoking new converts to seasoned believers. New converts are like a seedling that has just sprouted. They are fresh but fragile, and need time for their roots to grow down to ensure their faith is a robust one and not easily choked by thistles or stolen by birds (Matt 13:7). A new romance could easily stunt their growth in this crucial stage of development. To put it plainly, a new believer needs to fall in love with Christ before they fall in love with anyone else. Apply wisdom ... liberally!

Rebuilding Walls

Proverbs 25:28 "A person without self-control is like a city with broken-down walls."

A city without walls opens people up to ruin and destruction, and so does a relationship without boundaries. The nation of Israel came to ruin because they threw the "Boundary Book" out the window and tried to play by their own rules. In doing so they sacrificed their protection and peace and were tragically overrun by enemy nations who plundered their blessing and dignity. They were conquered from the inside out and found themselves bereft of national identity. In all the brokenness that ensued, they lost the very things that defined who they were.

Aren't you thankful that there is an entire book in your bible dedicated to rebuilding walls?

If you read the account of Nehemiah, rebuilding the walls of Israel was much, much more than an engineering project. It was about bringing order to chaos. It was about sweeping away national shame and restoring honour. It was about establishing authority and power for a bruised and weak people.[6] It was about moving from death to life. Building walls was seen as a life giving act – and when it comes to boundaries, it still is!

Wouldn't it be wonderful if we built strong, fortified walls in our relationships right from the beginning? Imagine if we protected our sexuality, body, mind, and heart with strong, healthy, organic boundaries so that by the time we stepped up to the altar, we knew the person standing opposite us was trustworthy to be granted access to *all* of us. What a celebration that would be! Maybe your walls have never crumbled – good for you! Keep them intact, and continue to be brave enough to say, "This far and no further, thanks."

But for those who have let their walls crumble like quicksand, Nehemiah's story fills us with hope for restoration. What makes Nehemiah's story so profound is not only the fact that he rebuilt something magnificent, restoring honour and identity to God's people – it's that he built in the face of hostile and *constant* persecution. In fact, each stage of his activity is met with some form of opposition. As the work progresses, the opposition becomes more fierce. As soon as the enemy hears that walls are being built, he lets loose with the discouragement to intimidate them into quitting. This strategy of intimidation is going to be a feature that keeps reappearing throughout the entire building process. Do not be surprised if the same thing occurs when you decide to build walls. The enemy will stand at the bottom of our walls and bombard us with Hollywood trends, pagan worldviews, and bullying taunts.

And here is the reason: the Enemy knows that rebuilding the walls leads to blessing. They separate us from the crowd and help define who we are. They restore our authority, honour, and identity. They protect our values, virtues and purity. If you're someone who has lacked boundaries in your relationships up until this point, there is absolutely nothing stopping you from picking up your tools and starting today. Everyone can enjoy the blessings that grow inside boundaries.

Isaiah 58:12 connects building walls with building a garden: "You'll be like a well-watered garden, a gurgling spring that never runs dry. You'll use old rubble of past lives to build anew the foundations from out of your past. You'll be known as those who can fix anything, restore old ruins, rebuild and renovate, make the community liveable again. You will be known as restorers and rebuilders!" (MSG)

If Israel could rebuild their broken down walls, so can you. In God's Kingdom, boundaries lead to blessings and His commands become promises. It's time we communicated our value in an all-access generation. Let's pave the way to well-watered gardens and flourishing relationships.

Dating in a Digital World

Now that we've covered that boundaries are actually a positive instrument that protects and leads to blessing, let's shift to the idea that we can take those boundaries and apply them to the activity of dating. But before we launch into what it means to date within a "digital age," we should probably attempt to define what dating actually *is*. As I briefly mentioned in the previous chapter, this is no easy task, because I don't know if you've noticed, but there is no *dating* chapter in the Bible. There's a *love* chapter (1 Cor 13). The bible certainly talks about relationship, betrothal, and even friendship … but not dating! The cultural setting of the Bible was arranged marriage, and the motivation for the decision was usually more economical than romantic. That's not to say romance didn't exist (hello, Song of Solomon) but the culture of dating we know in the West was not extant in the ancient Middle East. Typically, people married and *then* fell in love (aided by sexual intimacy which, for the Jewish person, was not previously experienced with anyone else but each other). In our Western culture, we approach it from the reverse by falling in love (whatever our criteria for this is) *then* getting married.

So if we're going to talk about dating, we have to acknowledge from the outset that we're speaking into a subculture that we've created in relatively recent centuries, and it's predominantly a Western sub-culture. It's a category that we've created between singleness and engagement that actually didn't exist in the biblical era. We've created an interim between singleness and betrothal, and it's getting larger and longer. Saving sex until marriage is becoming difficult for some because we're culturally pushing the age of marriage back further and further.

Is Dating Biblical?

You can comb the Scriptures from top to bottom, but you won't find people sitting across from each other in a candlelit restaurant trying to discern whether they're a suitable partner. They had a different process that was highly family-oriented in what we call an "honour-shame culture."[1] Thankfully we can rely on the timeless Word of God to transcend all cultures, Western or otherwise. "Dating" is an activity that we've developed in our Western culture that has become a part of our process. In our chapter on boundaries, we defined it as *the process of proving someone is trustworthy.* Trustworthy for what? To marry. If dating is the activity we choose to discern this trust, I suppose the question is not "is dating biblical?" but "is *your* dating biblical?"[2] I should ask the same question of any activities I participate in that aren't in the Bible. Is my surfing biblical? Am I abusing people out in the surf or am I having a good time? Is my driving biblical? Am I getting road rage and cutting people off, or am I taking care to drive responsibly and patiently? Just because an activity isn't specifically in the Bible, it doesn't mean that Scripture doesn't guide us in how to approach it.

In fact, dating has become complicated because we *haven't* used Scripture to define and constrain our approach to it. People concoct different labels and write books on dating, but no single book seems to answer all our questions because what dating means to *me* might be different to what dating means to *you*. It depends on where we came from, the environment we grew up in, our family of origin, what high school we went to. Do we call it dating or do we call it courting? Is it just hanging out or is it characterised by a formal date at a restaurant? Is it defined by the *titles* we place upon ourselves, like boyfriend and girlfriend? And by the way, who comes up with these sociocultural rules and gets to adjudicate them? People get hung up on labels but when we just come back to biblical principles and simple wisdom, a lot of that murky complexity is cleared up.

Rules for the Game

We might not initially associate the word "biblical principles" with the word "fun" but perhaps we associate the word "games" with fun. Every game – whether it's a board game, football, or Hide and Seek has a rulebook attached. Sometimes the rulebook is a tangible, tattered book you whip out of the board game box when you're highly suspicious of a move someone just made. Sometimes the rulebook is intuitive; it's not written down but we consciously know someone has committed some sort of infraction. Even my seven-year-old has a very keen intuition when she perceives a rule has been broken between her and her siblings: "But Mum, she's not playing *fair!*"

You see, boundaries define the rules and context for the game. Without them, anyone can do anything they feel like at any given time, and the game ceases to be a game. Can you imagine trying to play basketball without the boundary lines on the court, or an umpire? Without boundaries everything descends into chaos and there's no protection from selfish or dishonest people. It's never fun playing with a cheater. A cheater is someone who throws the rulebook out the window or redefines the rules to suit themselves. This is what has occurred in the Western quagmire of dating. Dating is not a bad activity, but if we try to play the game without a moral compass (or rulebook) it's not fun anymore. People have redefined it or abandoned it. As soon as we try to live without boundaries, mayhem and selfishness ensues. Many people in their heart of hearts are crying "that's not fair" but they have no rulebook to prove otherwise. Thank God we have access to the Book that gives us context for play: the Holy Scriptures. When biblical boundaries are in place, suddenly there is freedom to have fun. Psalm 16:6 says "The boundary lines have fallen for me in pleasant places, surely I have a delightful inheritance" (NIV).

Tridimensional Dating

The best part about having scriptural boundaries is that it accounts for our tridimensionality in the area of dating. Remember, dating is an activity we have developed to gauge trust in someone else. For this activity to be biblical, it must engage body, soul, and spirit. If we are tridimensional, it means our relationships are as well. The malady of our age is the attempt to separate the body from the soul as we muddle our way through dating and relating. Take online dating, for example. Online connections attempt to forge relationship without the involvement of our physical bodies. We connect through a screen, a text, an emoji, but not in person. This ultimately robs us, because authentic communion requires physical fellowship as much as emotional. Remember, this is a flesh and blood gospel. Our Jesus didn't wave a healing wand from heaven. He came to earth and physically touched people, ate with them, healed them and hugged them. Online connection has its place, but we also need flesh and blood communion. It's part of what makes us human.

Now, this isn't a penned protest against online dating. Like anything that isn't illegal or specifically unbiblical, we simply need to consider what we use it for and what appetite it feeds. There's no denying that social media and digital platforms feed our appetites for speed, giving us short relational attention spans. It grooms us to judge potential partners based on minimal information and appearance, instead of depth and character (virtues which can only be recognised from meeting organically and experiencing real life together).

It's not that we *want* to be superficial. It's just that dating apps provide us with *way* more romantic options than we could possibly date by trial and error in real life. We have no choice but to develop a process of elimination to sift through all the prospects, and usually that process is a reflection of social media itself: shallow and erratic. We end up scrolling through endless people like we scroll through our endless feeds. If we're not cautious, we can adopt a relational consumerism that imagines there's always a better romantic option if we pull the refresh button one more time or keep swiping. Statistically speaking, with the overload of options presented to us, that seems true. Except that it's not. A quick trip to the grocery store shows us that when we're presented with too many choices, it becomes only *more* difficult to make a decision, not less.

Cereal Dating

When I stand in the cereal aisle, I'm overwhelmed with the plethora of breakfast options available to me now. So many options tell me that my chance of making a *wrong* choice is much greater. What if there's a cereal that tastes better, or is healthier, or is cheaper, or lasts longer? So my eyes keep scrolling back and forth between all my options, and more times than I care to mention, I've walked out of the store empty handed. The "option overload" makes me superficially selective. But really, knowledge can't be gained from surface observation. It's gained from experience. If I actually tried the cereals, I'd have a greater chance of making the right decision. You know, get to know them over a leisurely Saturday breakfast. And hopefully, through an experiential process, I'll figure out which cereal is healthiest for me in the long run! But let's get out of the grocery store and back to dating: we simply cannot choose a partner based on the knowledge we get from digital platforms. That kind of knowledge is mostly arbituary and void of intimacy. Intimacy is a special kind of knowledge, and actually what the Bible defines as *true* knowledge. This kind of knowledge can only be gained from experiencing a person in the flesh, where you can look them in the eyes, watch them interact with their surroundings, see them express emotions … and, you know, figure out who will be healthiest for you in the long run!

All relationships have different levels of intimacy and exclusivity, based on context. Context is what drives body language, facial expressions, tone of voice, the amount we share and how we share it. For example, we will likely be more vulnerable and open with a close friend than a distant acquaintance. Social media unfortunately collapses all our relationships into *one* context: a digital platform. Platforms are a place where we're exposed to anyone who will look at us. It's a digital stage where we broadcast our thoughts and feelings – but it's bereft of intimacy and exclusivity. So, naturally, on the platform we're inclined to *perform*. And if you've ever watched a performer, there's always distance between the stage and the audience. You can't truly know a performer, you can only know a *person*. If we're going to date in a wholesome and healthy way, we're going to have to quit performing and jump off the digital stage that social media provides. But, we lament, how will we meet anyone if we're not on dating apps? We meet people the same way Christians have met one another for centuries. We meet on mission. Remember, humans have known how to make a connection far before we invented wifi!

Online connection might be a convenient *jumping off* point for connection, but it's not a great *decision* point.

Let's not be deceived though – before we were swiping left and right with our thumbs, we were prone to swipe in our minds. We were judging based on the wrong criteria long before smartphones came out. These digital bricks just exacerbated our Babel hearts and uploaded them for the world to see. Deciding on who to connect with, spend time with and who to trust is still God's domain. He is faithful to give wisdom in huge doses to those who faithfully ask for it (James 1:5). However, it's never too late, or too soon, to give our thumbs a break from scrolling and extend the hand of fellowship instead!

Friendship First

Dating might not be defined in Scripture, but there are two wide categories which are: singleness and marriage. Marriage is a covenant between two people, which includes expectations, promises (vows) and commitment. It has a time span – our whole lives. Singleness simply means "unmarried." Friendship is important because it encompasses both of these categories. In fact, the word for "friend" is a Hebrew covenant word, *chesed,* which is a sacrificial love that is usually translated into the English words "lovingkindness" or "mercy" in our Old Testament. Since friendship can be understood and honoured whether we're single or married, what if we prioritised friendship with someone before diving into an ambiguous "boyfriend" or "girlfriend" status with the person we're attracted to? It's probably a wise idea to drop the idea of "dating" for a moment and learn how to be a good friend before we learn to be a good lover. When we step up to the wedding altar we're going to want the person standing opposite us to be our *friend,* not a stranger, an enemy, or a random we met recently when we swiped right! We want to be sure that person will be a good companion and friend for life ... who isn't a golden retriever.

I know "friendship first" sounds boring and prudish to some, but friendship is indispensable because it's the foundation upon which all deeper relationships are built. If you're going to test whether this person is worthy of your heart, emotions, thought-life, time and energy, surely the greatest tester would be through the distiller of friendship.

The Myth of Soul Mates

There is much unnecessary pressure on the activity of dating in the West, in part due to our cultural idea of meeting our "soul mate." The soul mate issue is really a wrestle between God's sovereignty and our freewill. Does God in His sovereignty nail down one person for us to marry or does He let us choose anyone we want? This idea that there is *one* "Soul-Mate" out there floating around who we are destined to meet and marry is problematic because it can help justify affairs and divorce. If we hit a snag in our marriage and suddenly meet someone else who appears to tick all our boxes (and trigger all our hormones) we can say "I think I married the wrong person. Perhaps *this* person is my soul mate."

God is of course sovereign over your life but He doesn't pin down one person for you and then enforce you both to get together or else you're doomed to a life of loneliness and misery. The whole idea of a "soul mate" actually comes from Greek mythology, which believes you are half a soul and the other half of your soul is in another person out there.[3] Therefore, you have to find each other and when you do you become one *whole* person. However, this is not at all biblical. God makes us unmistakably whole and only He can bring us to wholeness when we're broken. He never made anyone with half a soul. Eve was a counterpart to Adam, but they were gloriously distinct from one another, with their own individual souls.

We like to believe in soul mates because the idea sounds romantic. Even if some of us don't favour the Greek mythology, sometimes we can still think there is the mystical "One" out there. But really, it's a disguised form of fatalism, leaving our marriage partner up to chance. God doesn't *make* our choices, He *shapes* our choices. Ever since the Garden, God has allowed humanity the gift of choice. It's the very reason He put a forbidden tree in Eden. It created the scenario where we actually get to *choose* or *refuse* relationship with God. Yes, He is sovereign, but God's foreknowledge of a choice doesn't mean He forces us to choose it.[4] He is not a cosmic puppeteer who controls us like creaturely machines – that's Babel territory.

As romantic as we think it sounds, this fear of missing out on finding "the One" actually eliminates our choice from the equation. As far as I know, there are only two occasions in the Bible when God tells a person to marry another.

#1 Hosea – God tells him to marry a prostitute to paint a picture of God's unfailing, faithful, never-giving-up-on-you love to a failing, faithless, always-giving-up-on-you humanity (Hosea 1:2).

#2 – He tells Joseph to go ahead and marry Mary because she's pregnant with, you know, the Messiah. It was kind of a one-off situation ... (Matthew 1:20)

The good news is, you're not an Old Testament prophet and the Messiah has already come – what a time to be alive! Jokes aside, even if we think an angel appeared to us and told us to marry someone, without choice love can't actually exist. Love is the supreme ethic that God has given us which places value upon the other person of worth, and you can never love without the freedom of choosing to do so. Despite the digital age we live in, we are not robots! If you're compelled like a machine to make a decision, you can never truly love. God won't force you to love Him, nor will He force you to love anybody else – let alone marry them.

True love is not defined by the level of attraction, amount of common ground we share, or even the burning passion we feel. True love is when people *choose* to love each other. Over and over again. Day after day. Who we elect as our marriage partner for life *becomes* "the One" at the altar. We better count the cost and ensure it's a wise decision before we make a life commitment. Jesus advised the same attitude before we made a covenant commitment to him in Luke 14:28. However, let me be clear that even when we make poor choices, God is all-knowing and there is not an inch of our lives His sovereign grace and redeeming work does not touch.

Becoming the One

The Bible might not use the phraseology of dating, romance, boyfriends or girlfriends, but it most certainly *does* deal with our relationships. Scripture doesn't say a whole lot about "how to find a great spouse" or "how to have the perfect first date." It might not tell me how to *find* a great person but it does instruct me on how to *be* a great person. Contrary to legalistic opinions, the Bible isn't about changing other people; it's about changing *you*. The common denominator of all your relationships, whether it's marriage, friendships, siblings, parents, teachers or pastors ... is you. So in a way, it does deal with our romantic relationships – it's just that Scripture is much more concerned with who we are *becoming* than who we are *finding*.

While it's beneficial to know what we want and value in a person, and of course crucial to uphold standards when it comes to choosing our partner, it doesn't give us permission to whip out the checklist every time we meet someone we like and make sure they tick all the boxes. If they don't, we put the checklist back in our pocket (or swipe left) and walk away, wondering why no one lives up to our expectations.

What if we flipped our focus from *finding* The One and instead focused on *becoming* The One? Rather than being on the hunt to find someone who meets our wants and needs, what if we endeavoured to become a great person? When I say a great person, I don't mean a perfect person. I mean someone who is spiritually and emotionally healthy and thriving. Before we attempt to find a healthy person, we would be wise to hold up a mirror and ask, "am *I* a healthy person?" Before we ask "how can I meet a healthy person to marry?" first we might ask "am I the kind of person someone healthy would *want* to marry?" Suddenly it becomes others-oriented, instead of self-oriented, and we move from Babel back to the Garden once again.

Maturity Matters

A healthy Christian is someone who is physically, emotionally, spiritually and sexually healthy. This is what we call "wholeness" and something the Bible explicitly deals with when it comes to humans. It's often the case that healthy people usually attract healthy people. With this in mind, if we pursue *becoming* a healthy person rather than *acquiring* a healthy person, we more likely *attract* a healthy person. Health is characterised by something that is alive, growing, fruitful and brings life to whatever is around it. The only plants that bear fruit in the garden are mature plants. By dictionary definition this means they are "fully developed or ripe ... completed natural growth of development ... stable growth."[5]

Song of Solomon takes us on a journey into the garden, deliberately laced with Edenic imagery and describing the journey of romance between two people. The presence of the *"Song of Solomon"* in the Bible shows us that God is not boring, prudish, or ashamed of sex and romance. The beauty of human sexuality is expressed without hesitation in this little not-so-G-rated book. Don't let the enamouring language fool you into missing the point: Song of Solomon is indeed about marriage, sex, relationships, romance, and the pursuit of lovers – but there is also a deeply poetic picture of the love between Christ and His Bride, the Church.[6] God uses a human couple to tell the story about Jesus and his love of humanity, and he does this by describing the way they love each *other*. I believe God wants to do the same with our love story, and if God exhales into your relationship with the same breath He used to inspire the Holy Scriptures, it *will* tell the world a great story. It won't be a story free from flaws or mess, but we can have marriages that tell stories of honour, faithfulness, intimacy, peace, kindness, romance, joy and infinitely much more.

Song of Songs 1:4 "Kiss me and kiss me again, for your love is sweeter than wine. How pleasing is your fragrance; your name is like the spreading fragrance of scented oils. No wonder all the young women love you! Take me with you; come, let's run! The king has brought me into his bedroom."

You might be able to see why young Jewish boys weren't allowed to read this book until they were of a certain age!

Rabbis had a point. There is a level of maturity you need to reach in order to not only read, but proverbially *write* this story with another person. To become "one flesh" and let your lives write these lyrics together, you need to be mature. "Mature" does not mean old, boring, passionless, and definitely not perfect. But there is a measure of spiritual, emotional, and physical maturity you want to look for in a partner (and ensure you've achieved personally) *before* you start singing the song of the Shulamite.

Physical Maturity

Age gaps are not as significant as you get older, but they certainly matter in our younger years. There is no black and white principle as to when we should start dating, but there is for when we should *not* start. By Western law, you have to be at least eighteen to get married, which provides a good marker for us in terms of when we are mature enough. Is there any point in dating at thirteen years old when we're nowhere near the age of getting legally married? It should not need to be said that someone needs to be of physical maturity before they enter into relationships and romance, but the age for dating is getting younger and younger as preteens engage in activities far beyond their years.

Song of Solomon deals with protecting the physically immature from older predators: "What shall we do with our little sister when men come asking for her? She's a virgin and vulnerable, and we'll protect her. If they think she's a wall, we'll top it with barbed wire. If they think she's a door, we'll barricade it" (MSG).

Emotional Maturity

Become and choose someone who is emotionally mature. Somebody who is able to keep their feelings in check (there are plenty of adults who have lived for decades on this planet and still don't know how to do this). How do we discern if someone is emotionally mature? Well, think about someone who is emotionally *immature*. They're lead by their feelings more often than their faith. They fly off the handle with a short temper. They create drama and thrive in it. Basically I'm describing an adult with a toddler mindset! You don't need to search for an emotionless robot (because that's actually another sign of emotional immaturity) but aim for someone who has grown in tempering their emotions with a good dose of faith and self control. Like a garden, a mature person has firm but flexible boundaries, not just for the sake of themselves but for others. Most importantly, they have integrity and the kind of character that can carry their calling.

Spiritual Maturity

In your mind, contrast a mature tree to a baby seedling. Compared to the robust strength of a mature tree, a little seedling is fresh and fragile. It needs lots of careful tending. It's too soon to tell whether it's going to last the distance and grow to maturity. Will it be scorched by the sun? Will it wither from lack of nutrition? Spiritually immature people are rarely ready to be in a relationship. They need more time to grow into a robust Christian before they leap into a relationship with someone else. A spiritually mature person is worshipping Jesus with their whole life, not just twenty-minute song segments on Sundays. They've made some distance with Him. Their tree has the fruit on it that brings life and benefit to those around them. They're firmly planted in the kingdom with roots that have grown down deep in Christ's love.

You don't need to be thirty to write your love story – but you do need to be mature! You might be attracted to someone, but don't let the next chapter be written until maturity has been established. We simply cannot evaluate all the elements of maturity with one paragraph on a dating profile. Time, conversation, and life experiences reveal someone's health. You can view a tree on a screen, but you can't see its roots. However, it's important to remember that searching for perfection is a symptom of Babel. Don't look for perfection – look for fruit. Jesus provides this good rule of thumb for identifying healthy people:

Matthew 7:16–17 "You can identify them by their fruit, that is, by the way they act. Can you pick grapes from thornbushes, or figs from thistles? A good tree produces good fruit, and a bad tree produces bad fruit."

Ripe Relationships

Building gardens means we don't approach relationships *structurally* (like a tower) but *seasonally*. It's in our nature to want to control, but relationships must be surrendered to the seasons. Gardens are subject to the seasons in a way that manmade structures are not, which means we have to allow them to go through (and grow through) different seasons before yielding certain results.

Have you noticed that we live in a generation where we want our fruit available all year round? Avocados are seasonal, but we want smashed avocado on toast and we want it available every day. So grocery chains make sure we get avocados every day! These days, modern farming practices involve injecting all manner of growth hormones into produce to make them grow bigger and faster.[7] Sure, they *look* impressive. They *look* like the real thing. But they don't have the *health* of the real thing. This process of quicker and impressive all-year-round availability actually strips them of their nutrients so we've got all of the appearances but none of the health. Sounds just like Babel to me.

By God's mercy, Christians will not image the surrounding culture of consumerism and apply it to the way we approach our relationships. There's something about alive, organic fruit that we cannot manufacture or manipulate. Our Babel human nature desperately wants to control the fruitfulness of other people – but whether we're talking avocados or my four-year-old, healthy relationships are not forced, but forged. We don't control, we cultivate. We tenderly foster an environment conducive to growth and life. What do you know? We're right back in the Garden once again, realising that our only option is to do it the way God asked us to do it *in the beginning!*

Like any plant, waiting for God's timing is crucial to the health of the relationship. When fruit is ripe to be picked, it simply drops from the tree. You don't have to pull, twist and rip it off the branch with a tight (or possessive!) grip. It drops all on its own with ease and grace, ready to be picked up and enjoyed. If your relationship is "ripe" to be picked and love ready to be "awakened" then the grace of God will allow it to happen. It won't require anyone's possessive grip, force, or haste.

Song of Solomon 8:4 "Oh, let me warn you, sisters in Jerusalem: Don't excite love, don't stir it up, until the time is ripe – and you're ready" (MSG).

Sometimes our feelings try and awaken something prematurely. Have you ever bitten into a fruit before it's ripe? It looks good, feels good, but doesn't taste right. Gross. Bitter. Leaves a chalky layer on your teeth. You kind of want to spit it out but that will look awkward in front of other people. But if we wait until the time and season is right – what a reward! Sweet to the taste and satisfying to our appetites (I'm still talking about fruit ...).

We're built with a relational hunger and if it's not fed with the right stuff (that is, our needs aren't getting met in a healthy way) we can begin to crave things that aren't so good for our soul. If you're that starving, it can make bitter things even begin to taste *good*. It can make unripe fruit seem like a legitimate snack. A toxic person could seem like a great candidate if we're that desperate. Making sure our soul is well-fed will help us deduce if our relationship and interaction with someone is "unripe" and "underdeveloped." You could say a full stomach is more "selective" and a full soul has higher standards!

Love is patient ... well, sacrificial love is. Romantic love is rather *im*patient. But God knows that there is a right time for everything we do in this life.

Ecclesiastes 3:1 "For everything there is a season, a time for every activity under heaven."

Relationships are as seasonal as your avocados, and they can only be yielded in the right time and season. If we're forcing a relationship to work prematurely, perhaps we need to press pause and assess our own maturity. Why the rush?

Fast Growth is Not Necessarily Good Growth

If we go back to Genesis, we already know God blessed the first man and woman, saying *"be fruitful and multiply."* When God's blessing is on your relationship, there's naturally going to be fruitfulness and multiplication. It will grow, but it doesn't necessarily grow rapidly. We want fast growth, but even within our body when cells grow and multiply too fast they grow unevenly, developing tumours which we call cancer. Cancer is the *counterfeit* of "be fruitful and multiply." Growth is meant to bring life, but cancerous growth brings death. Life comes to an end – and so do many relationships that move too quickly. They quickly mutate into something that would have otherwise been healthy if we had waited for the right time, applying wisdom and patience as we cultivated the relationship.

Digital dating may have some benefits, but immersing ourselves in its culture breeds relational impatience that accelerates the natural pace of a relationship. When communion takes place online, the pace quickens and natural stages of organic relationship tend to get skipped. Things like mustering up the courage to look someone in the eyes and have a rich conversation. Enduring awkward silences while we figure out how to communicate with one another. Reading body language and facial expressions. Watching how one another react and respond to unexpected interruptions and surprises. Some of these things might be uncomfortable, but so is weeding and fertilising. To bypass the unappealing aspects of gardening would be to forgo indispensable stages of cultivation.

Slow Growth is Not Necessarily Good Growth

On the flip side, the growth of a relationship need not be tediously slow either. This is what we call "stringing someone along." I'm personally not an advocate for long drawn out engagements that make it difficult for a couple to preserve sexual intimacy for marriage, or excuse them from making a commitment to one another. In this case, slow growth can be as harmful as rapid! Jesus cursed the fig tree in Matthew 11 because it was symbolic of Israel producing a whole lot of flashy proverbial "leaves" but no actual fruit. It was multiplying alright, but it wasn't yielding the kind of thing God actually designed it to produce.

To put it simply, healthy growth is *steady* growth. Growing healthy relationships is like cultivating a healthy garden; it takes time, tending, nurturing and patience. It requires us to surrender to the seasons, neither forcing a plant to fruit prematurely, nor waiting years for it to produce nothing but leaves. To borrow the words of Song of Solomon 8:4 once again: "Promise me, O women of Jerusalem, not to awaken love until the time is right…"

Cancel Culture

To summarise, we don't need our relationships to be fruitful *all* the time, just at the *right* time. For example, with a "Tower of Babel" mindset, barren seasons are equated to failure. The structure has failed because you're not producing results. On the other hand, the garden mindset knows that barrenness is merely a *season* every garden has to endure. Seasons change, and it's a natural part of the organic process of living things!

I wonder, if perhaps it is a departure from the garden mindset that contributes to the currently trending "cancel culture." Cancel culture is a modern form of ostracism where someone is shut down because they have said or done something considered offensive or objectionable. Those subject to this ostracism are said to have been "cancelled." The mindset behind it is a Babel mindset because it's centred on self-interest.

You failed *me* so I am officially *cancelling* this relationship.

My support of you: cancelled.

Friendship: cancelled.

Marriage: cancelled.

This culture isn't exclusive to the social media world but I certainly believe it's inflamed by it. In a digital world where relationships can often be characterised by image and speed and quantity – I wonder if the Church would be characterised by an entirely different way of doing relationship. To risk sounding cliche, what if our relationships were so resilient that the only thing we "cancelled" was the cancel culture? If we allow relationships the dignity of enduring seasons, we won't run when romance withers and the grass is greener in the neighbour's yard. Seasonal relationships endure the winters because they know spring is coming ... and these are the kind of relationships that yield fruit through the years, from generation to generation.

The Gift of Singleness

Are we destined to be married or are we called to be single? My hope for this chapter is that we begin to change the angle of this question. Firstly, since the word "destiny" implies a "destination", marriage in and of itself cannot be our ultimate destiny. As Christians we only have one of those and that is Heaven! Being single or married is a relationship distinction, not a destination. Our relational status is woven *into* our God-given destiny much like many other things, but it isn't the means to the end. If the Son of God could fulfil his destiny on earth as a single man, so can we! Paul the apostle fulfilled his God-given destiny as a single man, while Priscilla and Aquilla did so as a married couple. The point is, there is no need to pit marriage against singleness as though they are two opposing destinies. Marriage should continue to be esteemed, treasured, protected and aspired to, but we must never substitute our holy calling for it.

The only goal we should wholeheartedly be running towards as Christians is the heavenly calling as penned by (a single) Paul himself in Philippians 3:14: "I press on toward the goal to win the prize of God's heavenly calling in Christ Jesus." (BSB)

Over and against what some marriage seminars teach, Genesis 2:18 doesn't say "It is not good for man to be *single*," it says it is not good for man to be *alone*. Many have applied this scripture specifically to marriage but the words themselves speak about fellowship. We are intrinsically designed to need other people, yet this doesn't necessarily mean we need to be married to do so. So long as we're in communion with God and planted in the covenant community of the Church with other believers, we have all we need to walk out our God-given destiny. However, many people rightly desire marriage because of the unique intimacy and companionship it offers, including that of raising a family. As we discussed in chapter 1, if relationship is the vehicle through which God is building his Kingdom, than marriage is a noble goal and a valid desire.

Singleness is Not a Curse

Hopefully as we have read through the previous chapters (particularly chapter 4) we have recognised that marriage is an extraordinary gift. Not so many Christians will argue with this, but a great number forget that *singleness* is just as much of a gift. In fact, a well-known scripture which refers explicitly to singleness is 1 Cor 7:7 where Paul categorises it as exactly that: "Sometimes I wish everyone were single like me – a simpler life in many ways! But celibacy is not for everyone any more than marriage is. God gives the gift of the single life to some, the gift of the married life to others" (MSG).

Wow – according to Scripture, singleness is a "gift" handed out straight from the palms of God. The question now becomes "what is this gift, and how do I receive it?" There is nothing wrong with desiring companionship and romance, and I deeply empathise with those who feel like their season of singleness has extended way beyond it's use-by date! Yet I have witnessed so many young people rush through their season of singleness like it's a disease they need to rid themselves of. The question on their minds is "how do I become *un*-single?" as they frantically swipe left and right and scour online dating profiles. Instead of looking down at our phones, maybe we should look up, and ask: "God, what do you want to do in and through me as a *single* person?"

Missing the Moment

Being single is exactly what Paul implies here – it's special. While many are trying to crack the code of *leaving* their season of singleness rather than *receiving* from it, I firmly believe that there are purposes and gifts God desires to bring into our lives as single people that He simply cannot do once we are married or raising children. Some of the most powerful Christians I know are single people who carry PhDs, have mastered ancient Greek, or are devoted missionaries or incredible itinerant ministers. They are impacting their world in profound ways that carry deep eternal significance that could only be known in full once we're Heavenside. They're not sitting back on their haunches in cruise mode until romance strikes... no, they're using their season wisely and in a way that brings glory to God. Paul isn't trying to say married people *can't* achieve these things, but the pace and outworking of the calling will be vastly different. Essentially, he's taking the pressure off single Christians to sprint down the aisle in the name of his cultural norms and to instead prioritise the gospel mission! His inspiration comes from Jesus himself in Matthew 6:33 "Seek the Kingdom of God *above all else*, and live righteously, and he will give you everything you need" (emphasis mine).

Marriage and family are wonderful gifts to steward, but with it we have to accept the manyfold responsibilities and an entirely different lifestyle. Among many things, singleness provides us with the unique opportunity for undistracted devotion to God, allowing him to do deeply formative and transformative work in a way that would take more time (or be outright impossible) in other seasons of our lives. There is a reason Paul wrote "I wish that all of you were as I am" (1 Cor 7:7).

The Witness of Contentment

Sometimes people become so enamoured by the benefits they believe marriage will bring them, that they miss what God wants to do in their present. We would deeply regret missing out on the benefits of our present season by sacrificing them on the altar of an unknown future. One of the most powerful things we can pray is not "please give me x, y, z" but "make me content in every season."

Phil 4:11 "I am not saying this because I am in need, for I have learned to be *content* whatever the circumstances …" (NIV, emphasis mine). The word *content* here means to be fully satisfied with things as they are! Whether we're single or married, being relentlessly discontent is a symptom of the Babel epidemic. To be content in all circumstances is not only a powerful prayer, but an undeniable witness of a gospel that wholly satisfies.

The Lost Art of Preparation

Believe it or not, singleness is perhaps the most vital season of your life when it comes to marriage. What we do (or don't do) in our season of singleness forms the building blocks that our marriage will one day stand upon. It allows us the opportunity to lay crucial foundations in our lives before romantic feelings come along and hijack the wheel, steering us in a direction

God may not want us to go. Many people don't start thinking about laying relationship foundations until they're interested in or already pursuing someone, but this is probably not the best time to do this. As we explored in chapter 5, romance is intoxicating and it's much easier to make wise choices if you pre-decide on them beforehand. You know, when you are in a more "sober" condition!

Since *you* are the common denominator in all the relationships you will ever have, the best way to set yourself up for success in the area of romance is to prepare your*self*. This is by no means restricted to the area of relationships. We prepare for many things we value in life. Every recipe for a good meal has a "preparation time" preceding the "cooking time." Expectant couples go to great lengths to set up their baby nursery with a cot, changing table, nappies and tiny baby clothes, all before the baby comes. Long distance runners might desire to win the gold, but that desire is redundant if they don't actually prepare to win by consistent training. It's one thing to sign up for a race, but it's an entirely other thing to prepare for it.

It's evident that if we truly want to succeed and flourish in something, we go to the effort (even pains) to ready ourselves. However, for whatever reason, many seek to bypass their season of singleness and skip straight to the altar without training for the marathon of marriage! "Pre" means "before, previous to." *Pre*paration takes place before the event at hand, so it stands that the ideal time to train ourselves for successful marriage occurs *pre* the wedding altar! Singleness gives us the opportunity to prepare. It affords us the time to allow God to develop and fashion our heart, mindset, attitudes, lifestyle and friendships. Contrary to what some might believe, they don't hand out magical discipline dust with your wedding certificate. Learning self-control and sacrifice is crucial prior to marriage, because it is very much needed once you're in it! In this way, we prepare to actually keep the promises we will make one day to that special person at the altar.

Building Foundations

Let us for a moment imagine a house, and that house represents your marriage. Every house is built upon a foundation, even though it is the part you can't see. My dad happens to be a builder, and when I asked him about the process of building a house, he immediately replied *"The foundation takes the longest to build."* Curious, I asked why. *"Because it's the most critical part. Everything else about the house can ultimately be fixed if you make a mistake ... but if you build a house on top of a foundation that you didn't lay correctly – it's almost impossible to rectify it."*

Why does the foundation matter so much? According to the builder, a foundation that hasn't been laid correctly throws the entire level of the house out. Everything else you attempt to build from thereon will be a huge struggle. Every wall you try to build is going to be compromised if the foundation is slightly off. And if your foundation is weak and unstable? It doesn't actually matter how good the style of the house is, how pretty the bench tops are, how expensive the appliances are, whether you dressed it in the latest technology ... the entire house could still fall down.

Foundations matter, whether we're patient or not. At the end of the day, no matter how attractive our partner is, how anointed they are or how great their job is, if we don't build our relationship with them on a solid foundation the whole thing could still crumble. If we attempt to date someone without first laying solid foundations in our single life, we will end up dating on unstable ground. Our life and heart might not have the structural integrity to handle a relationship, and when the house crumbles, everyone inside gets hurt.

Singleness is a great foundation-laying time for your life. It is the most critical part of this whole process of building relationships, and because of this, it takes some time. Laying the foundation is not something you want to rush through as a builder. Sure, you can cut a few corners when you're laying the carpet or painting the inside walls. But the foundation is crucial to the integrity of the house, and so it is relationally: the foundation you lay in your single years will become crucial for your marital years. By the time you reach the wedding day and begin to build upon this foundation, you want it to be strong, stable and true. Can you see why singleness is such a wonderful gift? God has given us the gift of *time* for something critical that *takes time*. It is no different to building a garden. Much of the structural integrity happens underground, where the root system keeps the plant upright and stable. Impatient gardeners want to see the seed breakthrough, but if they rushed the underground process it would compromise the stability and health of the plant. Whether we're talking plants or houses, the strength of it is in what was built underneath. If you desire a strong marriage, build wisely in your single season. Don't squander a good gift!

The Foundation of Biblical Convictions

When we're single, we have the gift of opportunity to discover and develop what we truly value. Do you value Jesus Christ and his Church? Do you value the calling of God, using your spiritual gifts and fulfilling His purpose for your life? Do you value sexual purity and safeguarding it to present it as an exclusive gift to your future spouse? Do you value family and raising children who will walk in the ways of the Lord? Identifying these convictions takes a little time, experience and maturity. When I was fourteen I childishly thought it would be super important to marry someone who surfs. However, after a little bit of life and experience, I realised that it was of course not a deal-breaker for me! I discovered that what was really important for me in a relationship was spending my life with someone who is kind, honest, encouraging, and uncompromisingly devoted to Jesus. As I delved into my Bible and matured in my perspective, I learned that it was much more important to be with someone who was not only going to be a great husband, but who would be a great father to my children and disciple them alongside me in the ways of Jesus. Hobbies, looks, and taste in food come secondary to these things. Physical attraction is of course important for a relationship, but keep in mind that someone's looks won't raise your children – their mind and heart will.

Taking time to discover what is important to you and letting Scripture shape and determine these values is vital to creating a happy home in the future. Sure, opinions and perspectives change over time, but convictions are different. We can be assured that the kind of convictions that will not shift or erode with time are the ones found in the Bible, and if we draw our relational values from the timeless pages of Scripture they will still hold true whether we're 18 or 88! For some, this process takes many years. For others, the timeline is shorter and they have decided what they deeply value before they graduate high school. Western culture tends to underestimate our young people's ability to make profound and permanent decisions. I know Christians who wed at twenty, nineteen, and even eighteen, benefiting from growing in God together because they were prepared adequately for healthy relationships in their teenage years. I wonder if Babel culture is pushing the age of marriage back further and further because the *maturity* level is being pushed back further and further. Perhaps we aren't providing the adequate *preparation* for dating, marriage, and sex, in those formative teenage years when it really counts, and so we're finding many thirty year olds have the relational maturity of fifteen-year-olds. The Bible doesn't put a timeline on how long maturity should take and neither will I. The point is not so much the amount of time it takes us, but whether we have used our season of singleness to identify these foundational ingredients!

The Foundation of Biblical Boundaries

Once we unearth what we truly value in a relationship, we protect those convictions with boundaries. (We examined this more comprehensively in chapter 7.) Singleness is the prime time to learn what boundaries are and set them firmly in place so those values are protected. It's not ideal to attempt this when you're already in a relationship, because our feelings of attraction can deceive us and try to steer us. It is a part of being human to have intense feelings, but if we don't have a plan in place, we end up being *led* by those feelings. Feelings make terrible drivers, since they're fickle and subject to change. For example, if you're attracted to someone who isn't a believer but you have pre-decided that being equally yoked is something you value, than you can give yourself permission to ignore your feelings. If you don't feed them, they'll eventually fade and we can surely trust the Holy Spirit to sanctify our desires, especially our romantic ones!

Inside of a romantic relationship, unless we have *pre*-decided on what we value and *how* we're going to protect those values, we will likely give in to compromise. What does compromise mean? It's settling for something you *don't* believe in because you're unwilling to fight for what you *do* believe in. Our singleness is where we get to build our "fighting" muscles so that once we're in a romantically or sexually charged environment, we've got some strength and muscle to fight for those convictions and values! If we lack the foundation of convictions and boundaries, our feelings and hormones will drive us where we don't want to go and we're bound to have some head-on collisions.

The Foundation of Biblical Friendship

We need not prepare for marriage via a string of painful break-ups. Contrary to the advocates for serial dating, people are not platforms upon which we must train for marriage. *Friendship* is. Can we build friendship with someone we have romantic feelings for? Of course. You can be friends with all kinds of people. The Bible doesn't teach us how to date someone – it teaches us how to love someone. And we can love anyone with a sacrificial, friendship love. Befriending someone, and eventually committing to courtship (rather than playing with their feelings to make us feel good) is how you love someone well. It's how you place dignity and respect upon someone, even if you decide you no longer want to pursue them romantically.

Learning to flourish in your friendship is significant because the way you approach your friendships is a reflection of how you will approach marriage one day. If we don't learn to be a good friend now, we'll probably make a lousy spouse later. One day when the honeymoon stage has worn off, we will treat our spouse in a similar way that we treat our friends. Whether or not we learned sacrificial love, selflessness, honour and integrity in our single years will come to light. That's not to say we can't learn this at any point in life, but it's much wiser to train for a marathon *before* we enter a race rather than half way through. Rather than the consumerist method of "serial dating" and casual flings, the best way to train for marriage is learning to be a wonderful and godly friend.

When a Foundation Fails

If a house has bad foundations and cracks, it gets "condemned." Maybe some of you have come across a condemned house before. It usually has a sign across it declaring *"condemned property, do not enter."* It's a legal message announcing that no one is allowed to live here or come onto this property because it's too dangerous. Everything might look good from the outside, but a faulty foundation doesn't pander to externalities. A house might boast the most expensive furniture and latest technology on the inside, but if the foundation cracks it's still a danger to others.

In a sobering way, if we attempt to build our relationships on faulty foundations, it risks becoming condemned territory. There's a loss of relationship and no one is allowed back there because it carries the risk of pain and loss. We often see this with bad breakups. Previous couples can't even be in the same room anymore, let alone remain friends. The relationship is now *condemned* territory.

Getting the foundation right from the start not only protects us from the pain of a home that falls apart, but the children that may one day live under that roof. Perhaps this is time to remind ourselves that our relationships are not only about *us*. Whether we're reading this as a fresh-faced teen or broaching 30, we owe it to our future kids to get this right. Now, there is no part of our lives that the scarred hand of Jesus cannot reach into, and that includes crumbling marriages. If we've built on a faulty foundation he can make it right, but it will require painfully bulldozing what we've built and starting from scratch. We're much better off taking the time to use this vital gift of singleness to lay a strong, stable foundation *before* beginning to build a relationship with someone.

Spiritual Bridesmaids and Groomsmen

In chapter 4 we explored the idea of covenant in ancient Jewish culture and the role of the maid of honour and best man. We still uphold the tradition of having groomsmen and bridesmaids at our wedding, but in Jewish antiquity they served a purpose that went far beyond the wedding day. The bridesmaids were quite literally *maids* to the *bride*. A maid is another term for "servant" and this is exactly what they were for. They served the bride-to-be during her time of betrothal by helping prepare her for marriage! The groomsmen did likewise with the groom, serving him and helping him get his things in order for marriage.[1] Back then a girl could be betrothed for a year or more before the actual wedding day. In fact, the bride did not know the date of her wedding; she had to wait until her groom surprised her in the night! When he did so, he would come down the street with his groomsman, ringing bells and carrying lanterns in a glorious hubbub, while people in the village trickled out onto the streets and joined the festivities. Jesus grabs hold of this cultural picture when he tells the parable of the ten virgins and teaches people about – you guessed it – *preparation*. The whole parable is about being in a state of preparation, because you don't know when the Bridegroom (Jesus) is going to spring himself upon you. He will come *"like a thief in the night"* the Bible says. His Jewish audience of course understood this analogy clearly!

In the same way, singleness provides us with the opportunity to move ourselves into an appropriate state of preparation. No, this does not mean compiling the wedding Pinterest board or scouring online dating profiles for the perfect match. However, you never know when the right kind of person will spring up in your life unannounced. If and when they come, will we be prepared? Will we be the right person for them? Hopefully we have seen by now that preparation for marriage is about keeping our lamp lit with the Holy Spirit, protecting our purity and values and laying a firm bedrock to build a happy home upon. It's about becoming a spiritually and emotionally healthy person. As we close this chapter it is worth asking ourselves: who are my bridesmaids and groomsmen? It is of indispensable value to surround ourselves with friends and family who will prepare us for marriage by championing our purity and health. We need a village of people who will stick by us like glue (and vice versa) and encourage us to run from lust and pursue holiness. Do I have friends who will *serve* this purpose in my life, and will I do the same for them? Those are the kind of bridesmaids and groomsman we want in our life.

At the end of the day, we cannot prepare ourselves in our own strength. Our efforts (and our friends') will fall short no matter how hard we try, if we're not living in the grace of God. Jesus Christ has left us the ultimate Bridal Party to keep close by our side: the Word of God and his Holy Spirit. In fact, in Jewish antiquity there was one man who was designated "The Bridegroom's Friend" who negotiated the marriage between both parties.[2] The Holy Spirit is our ever-present Friend to prepare us, strengthen us, keep us accountable and guide us as we spend our singleness laying rock solid foundations for a future filled with hope.

Jeremiah 29:11 "For I know the plans I have for you," says the Lord. "They are plans for good and not for disaster, to give you a future and a hope."

Babel's Table

Whether we're single, dating or married, one of the greatest hurdles to overcome is grappling with sexual and relational appetites. An 'appetite' is essentially the desire to satisfy a need. What gets us into trouble is when we attempt to meet those desires in a way that is immoral, harmful, or unhealthy. Many *want* to live the right way, they *want* holy habits, they even want to *want* the right thing – but feel bound by cravings for forbidden fruit! Fortunately, this is by no means a foreign topic in Scripture and something salvation engages with directly. The freedom Jesus offers sets us free from bondage to our lustful cravings; we no longer have to be controlled by Babel appetites. One of the greatest gifts of the gospel is the redirecting and sanctifying of our desires. To 'sanctify' something is to make it holy and whole. Yes, Jesus offers us the kind of transformation that takes our "I have to's" and turns them into "I want to's". We might read Psalm 37:4 from this angle: "Take delight in the LORD, and he will give you your heart's desires." This doesn't necessarily mean God *grants* us what we want but *transforms* what we want. Healing the blind and lame is an outrageous miracle, but never overlook one of the most miraculous aspects of salvation: the healing of our desires.

Salvation: Not an Overnight Sensation

We've discussed in previous chapters the perils of reducing sexuality and dating to a one-dimensional experience. What is surprising however, is that Christians sometimes reduce our salvation to a one-dimensional experience! *"Getting saved will solve all your problems."* From an eternal perspective this is quite true, but this attitude reduces our salvation to a purely spiritual experience, when in fact it is tridimensional in nature. This means that salvation not only engages our spirit, but also our body and soul. In the Gospels there is a word used interchangeably for both salvation and healing, which is the Greek word "*sozō*". It's best translated as "*wholeness*". Salvation involves God restoring us back to the wholeness we cherished in the Garden. You know, before that serpent convinced us that the forbidden fruit would taste better. Perhaps no one knew this better than Paul, who writes in 2 Thessalonians 5:23 "Now may the God of peace make you holy in every way, and may your whole spirit and soul and body be kept blameless until our Lord Jesus Christ comes again."

Needs of the Body

Whether we know it or not, our desires are connected to our needs. Since we're tridimensional creatures, it makes perfect sense that we are created with needs that impact all three aspects of our being. Every human has physical, spiritual, and psychological needs. This is *why* we have appetites! An appetite is an inner drive that motivates us to ensure a need will be met. There is nothing shameful about our unmistakable neediness as creatures; it preaches a resounding message that humans are utterly dependent on our Creator. Our hunger points us to the only One who can fully and endlessly satisfy: God.

The needs of the body are relatively obvious. To stay alive, we need basic things like food, water, shelter, sleep and exercise. If these requirements are not met, the need becomes irrational. An irrational need leads to desperation, where our initially *normal* desire can distort into an unholy *craving*. For example, physical hunger is an entirely normal need. Everyone gets hungry and everyone tries to find a way to get fed – even newborns instinctively cry to ensure their bellies are full! However, if we don't meet our hunger in a healthy way with substantial food, that hunger can become irrational. Our "appetite" (the drive to meet that need) can distort to the point where we indulge in junk food that diminishes our health. If hunger is left unchecked even further beyond this point, people turn to outrageous ways to meet the need. They begin to crave and lust after things they would never have dreamed of. There are even true stories of starving people who have turned to cannibalism to appease their desperate appetite! On a more realistic level, we daily experience how unmet physical needs affect us spiritually. If our physical need for enough sleep isn't met, we're more irritable and likely to sin by giving into a short temper or speaking curtly. We also get frustrated and even irrational if we're really hungry (this is what we call being *hangry*). Indeed, food (especially carbs) stabilise our moods and help us make better decisions. You might remember 1 Kings 19 when the great prophet Elijah was burnt out and depressed. God ministered to his physical needs before attending to anything else, granting him sleep (v5), food (v6), and a quiet, rejuvenating space (v9). When it comes to having a healthy and moral sexual appetite, one of the wisest things we can do is eat well, sleep well and exercise! We are less likely to give into sexual temptation if our physical needs are healthily satisfied and stress is minimised.

Needs of the Spirit

The needs of our spirit are quite different. Our spirit requires reconciliation and communion with God, fellowship with other believers and continual meditation on Scripture. Jesus referred to our spiritual need when he proclaimed "I am the bread of life. Whoever comes to me will never be hungry again. Whoever believes in me will never be thirsty" (Jn 6:35).

If these needs aren't met, our spiritual hunger will mutate into something sinful. We might attempt to appease our starving spiritual appetite with other religions, cults, the occult or false doctrine. Remembering the word "Babel" meant "gate of the gods" to the Babylonians, but in Hebrew it meant "confused."[1] Among many things, the Tower of Babel is well known to be linked to astrology and counterfeit religion. It's no surprise that the New Age religion is on the rise as spiritually ravenous seekers attempt to find purpose, destiny, and salvation in confusing counterfeit ideas!

God may have attended to Elijah's physical needs, but it's important to note that He also ministered to him spiritually. Verse 5 tells us an angel touched him in the midst of his brokenness and need. Friends, if we want to be sexually whole, we need the Spirit and presence of the Living God. We need a touch from God through his Word and through worship. We need a spiritually rejuvenating space called church. These are the means through which God ministers to us and meets our spiritual needs. If we crave things or people we shouldn't, we need to examine our devotional life. Is it time to get our face out of Facebook and into the only Holy Book that will transform us? Perhaps if we paused long enough to stop touching those glass screens, we'd receive a touch from God!

Needs of the Soul

It could be argued that it is the needs of our soul that are exposed the most in the arena of relationships. It is a basic human need to receive love, affirmation, affection, and companionship. If these needs aren't met in a healthy way, our desires will distort and we begin to crave sinful and toxic methods to appease our emotionally malnourished appetites. For example, people who don't have their needs met in a *healthy* family context tend to find themselves in *unhealthy* relationships, attempting to get an intense emotional need met by way of a harmful shortcut. Those who are starved for attention might develop an unhealthy appetite for getting noticed, using their body or phone (or both!) to satisfy a psychological need. Perhaps you've been desperate for companionship, so you've engaged in gossip to secure an easy connection with a potential friend. Gossip meets the need for connection quickly, but it's not an authentic connection and will only result in an insecure friendship. The ends justify the means, so to speak, and we're all tempted to do this to various degrees in life.

Elijah had exerted tremendous emotional energy before burning out. He'd experienced the height of ministry success as he preached and performed miracles on Mount Carmel. (It's interesting to observe that many pastors who have fallen morally, do so during burn out that follows ministry success). But possibly the most draining for Elijah was having his high hopes dashed as Israel still didn't repent and revival didn't break out after all his ministering. By the time he crashed under a broom tree, he was disappointed and broken hearted. Emotionally drained, his desire distorts into something tragic: "I have had enough, LORD," he said. "Take my life..." (1 Kings 19:4b) Did Elijah really desire to die, or was his emotional and psychological needs acutely unmet? Before correcting or even speaking to him, God responds by meeting all his tridimensional needs.

A broken heart makes us greatly vulnerable to sexual or relational sin. Many emotional or sexual marital affairs begin with an already broken heart that was never healed. It's so important that we ensure God has healed our brokenness before entering a romantic relationship. If our heart isn't healed, we'll attempt to use the person to heal our emotional and psychological wounds in ways that only Jesus can. We'll look to our partner as our saviour, expecting them to be our anchor of security, identity, approval, attention, and acceptance. Though we should expect some of these things to a reasonable degree from our partner, no romantic relationship can achieve what Psalm 147:3 declares of God alone: "He heals the brokenhearted and bandages up their wounds."

Distorted Desires

Let's not pretend any of this is a modern issue. Appetites have been getting us into trouble since the Garden! As we discussed in the first chapter, Adam and Eve's appetite drove them to eat the forbidden fruit, in direct rebellion to God. But it was also a misdirected appetite – they attempted to meet their desire by any means necessary. In God's Kingdom, the end does not justify the means. Taking shortcuts to fill our appetite gives birth to Babel.

Perhaps James was considering this process when he penned the words "These desires give birth to sinful actions. And when sin is allowed to grow, it gives birth to death" (Jas 1:15). The word for "desire" here is *epithymia* (ἐπιθυμία) which describes a lustful craving. James is describing a *distorted* desire.[2] Humanity is born with an appetite bent toward sin, but salvation in Christ redirects it towards the holy target. However, even once saved, if our basic human needs are not met physically, psychologically, and spiritually, we develop warped appetites that send us running back to Babel. Even the Israelites were tempted to run back to Egypt after their mighty deliverance from slavery under Egyptian rule. They began to crave the leeks, onions, and meat from Egypt as soon as their stomachs grumbled in the wilderness! (Num 11:4–6) Part of becoming whole entails acknowledging where our needs have not been met and allowing Christ to show us how to meet them healthily. A "misdirected" appetite means it is aimed in the wrong direction. It is not wrong to have a desire, but the desire deforms into sin when we aim at the wrong thing to meet it. As it turns out, the Greek verb for "sin" is *hamartanō* (ἁμαρτάνω) which is an archery term for when one misses the target.[3] The Word of God helps us aim our desires in the right direction, like an arrow hitting the bullseye. (You might say the Holy Spirit is the wind that blows the arrow in our favour!) Remember, Luke 6:21a records a promise that pertains to our appetites: "God blesses you who are hungry now, for you will be satisfied."

Knowledge vs Wisdom

We are living in a digital age where we have access to infinite knowledge quite literally at our fingertips. Our generation worships knowledge but it must be asked, is it making us any better? Is it satisfying and edifying us, or is it simply bloating us with information, as Paul warns us of in 1 Cor 8:1? "… this 'knowledge' puffs up, but love builds up" (NIV).

Our generation recites a global hymn *"Knowledge is Power"* but is it the right kind of power? If you remember, it was the tree of "knowledge" in the Garden that got us into trouble in the first place. What we need is wisdom to learn how to *apply* knowledge in a way that leads to life and fruitfulness.

When we're hungry or thirsty our body manifests signals that tell us there is an unmet need. Salivation, a rumbling belly or even hunger pangs if it's 4pm and all we've had is a double shot flat white. When we're experiencing these signals, we seek to appease our appetite. *Knowledge* tells us what options are available to meet our need. Knowledge is knowing the fridge is full of cake, energy drinks, chocolate bars, fruit, vegetables, and a healthy sandwich. *Wisdom* is the ability to discern what option we should choose to meet that need in a way that leads to life, health and fruitfulness. (Hint – it's not the chocolate bar!) You might easily recognise the signals of your stomach, but great wisdom lies in learning to discern the signals of your soul. The soul manifests symptoms such as impure thoughts, outbreaks of lust, selfish desires, addictive habits, anger and even violence. The deeper our need, the stronger our drive to meet it. The stronger our drive, the lower our standards drop while we decide what will do the trick. For our true blessing, satisfaction, and all-around health, it's crucial that we dine at the right table.

Babel's Table

The book of Proverbs contrasts two opposing appetites, pictured appropriately by dining at two different tables. One is what I call the "Babel Table" and we are invited there by someone the writer calls "Woman Folly."[4] Now before the women bristle in defence, Woman Folly is not an attack on either gender. She is simply the personification of Lust, the Queen of Babel, and she can rule the mind of males and females alike. The writer in 9:13–14 describes her as a sexually promiscuous harlot, loud, immoral, and seductive, who "… sits at the door of her house, on a seat at the highest point of the city" (NIV).

Lust is in charge of Babel's Table, and little effort needs to be made to get our needs met there. She will willingly lead you up the steps into her tower via seduction or coercion. People get drunk at her banquets, intoxicated on the luxury and excesses of the world, lowering our inhibitions so we can no longer discern between right and wrong. Did you notice where she sits? The *"highest point"* in the city is not just geographical elevation, but social exaltation.[5] She's popular in a mainstream, crowd-pleasing kind of way. According to Proverbs, there is an outcome for dining at Babel's Table: eventual death and destruction.

Hollywood is the same popular harlot dressed in a modern outfit. She hisses loudly, attempting to seduce us into making the same mistake Adam and Eve did in the Garden: Satisfy your cravings with forbidden fruit! Get your needs met the fastest way possible, even if it means choosing temporary release over eternal truth. Gratify your desires no matter who or what gets hurt in the process. If you didn't catch on from her name, "folly" is a word synonymous with "foolish, absurd, reckless, lack of foresight, insanity..."[6] There is a message for those considering dining at Babel's Table: it's stupid! We may not experience literal death, but She will destroy our relationships before our bellies are full. Oh, didn't I mention? You can't get full at her table anyway. Ecclesiastes 6:7 describes what your dining experience will be like: "Everyone's toil is for their mouth, yet their appetite is never satisfied" (NIV).

Wisdom's Feast

Thank God there is another meal option. In fact, it's the first one we're presented with in the book of Proverbs: Woman Wisdom. She's portrayed as true, righteous, noble, and virtuous.[7] She's got a table too, but it stands in stark contrast to the shameless revelry at Babel's Table. She won't bully or entice you to come – She will simply call out a clear invitation to all (Prov 1:20) with no prejudice, no RSVP, no dress code, and no disqualifications. It means anyone can come and feast at her table, and unlike Babel's Table, it's the only place we will find satisfaction for the soul. Yes, the needs of our body, soul and spirit can be wholly satisfied! If Babel's Table leads to death, there is a sure reward for feasting at Wisdom's Table: *Life*. As we discussed in chapter 3, Isaiah 55:1–2 echoes the call to this Banquet:

"Is anyone thirsty? Come and drink – even if you have no money! Come, take your choice of wine or milk – it's all free! Why spend your money on food that does not give you strength? Why pay for food that does you no good? Listen to me, and you will eat what is good. You will enjoy the *finest food*. Come to me with your ears wide open. Listen, and you will find *life*" (emphasis mine).

Wisdom's Table is full of fruit straight from the Garden, and it's the kind of fruit that brings nourishment to our soul, vitality to our lives and satisfaction to our relationships. If you haven't dined at this table, you can go ahead and assume your soul is hungry and thirsty. But if you've been filling up at Babel's Table, you'd be none the wiser. If we're in the habit of meeting needs in unholy ways, we can forget that we're even hungry. When I've appeased my belly rumblings with cheeseburgers and chocolate, I no longer feel hungry – but I somehow don't feel satisfied either. Often, we don't think to even make a change in our diet until we fall sick from malnutrition.

Getting Our Appetite Back

So, what's the remedy when we've lost our holy appetites? Sometimes we have to starve our fleshly appetites to awaken our hunger for the Bread of Life. It's no wonder God fed the Israelite's flatbread for 40 years while they were learning to quit their cravings for Egypt. He was shaping their appetites as His holy people, both physically and spiritually (Exodus 16). Sometimes this requires us to starve ourselves of certain things until our appetite has been reshaped and redirected. We might initially recoil at this thought, but let me remind you that sacrifice is at the very heart of our entire faith. The cross is not something we simply dangle around our necks as a piece of iconography – it's something we proverbially pick up daily and apply to every way we live. Besides, there is nothing better than an appetite that hits the bullseye. It's like drinking fresh water after realising you've been swallowing saltwater for years, wondering why you've never successfully quenched your thirst. At Wisdom's Table, you can be assured there is fresh water and a banquet to die for.

Awakening the Wrong Appetite

If we're wrestling warped appetites, have confidence in this: when it comes to our desires, distorted or otherwise, whatever appetite we feed will grow. Whatever appetite we starve will shrink. Have you noticed that whenever you watch a cooking show or scroll through Foodstagram, it somehow awakens an appetite in you that was definitely not there when you began? You were happily satiated until you watched a pastry chef bake a delicious brownie oozing with chocolate sauce. Suddenly, you need chocolate. Your appetite for sugar has been awakened and you find yourself rummaging in the back corners of the pantry at 10pm at night (I could possibly be speaking from personal experience …).

Shameless confessions aside, the point is this: If I am trying to build healthy habits in my life when it comes to food, I won't be looking at meals that are bad for me on screens or recipe books. Let's say I'm a diabetic and having certain amounts of sugar could risk my life – I may even need to refrain from socialising with people who influence me to eat bad food until I've built healthy habits and become used to my new diet. This makes sense to us on a physical level, and we'd be wise to apply this to our souls as well, especially in the area of sexual and emotional health. The community of people we surround ourselves with is extremely important when it comes to renewing the mind and creating new habits. That includes digital community – if the eyes are the window to the soul, then social media will present us with a *feast* for the eyes, but it's one that can give you food poisoning. We might fellowship with healthy people in real life, but don't realise we're hanging out with Woman Folly online. Our mind is being influenced by the religion of Babel as we scroll excessively, often late at night when our minds are most vulnerable.

Wholeness requires us to starve ourselves of things that awaken an unholy appetite. Scroll with caution, friends. When we do, our holy cravings for the One who fully satisfies will begin to blossom ... and so will we.

Psalm 1:2–3 "Instead you thrill to God's Word, you chew on Scripture day and night. You're a tree replanted in Eden, bearing fresh fruit every month, Never dropping a leaf, always in blossom" (MSG).

An Appetite for Life

Really these two tables are juxtaposing two different kingdoms: One of the World and one of the Christ. Babel's kingdom or The Garden Kingdom. One of the most glorious aspects of salvation is the healing and sanctifying of our desires. He sets us free from *deformed* desires by *transforming* our inner appetites.

Anyone who has failed a New Year's resolution to eat healthy will tell you that this is not an overnight change. Appetite transformation takes time, consistency, discipline, and a constant surrender to the Holy Spirit in our lives. The reward? An appetite for *life* and not death! Oh how free it truly is to crave godliness and godly things – to actively desire things, habits and people that bring us life, not death! To desire fresh fruit from God's Garden, not stale crumbs from Babel's Table. Gritting our teeth, listening to back-to-back podcasts and sheer willpower will not bring about this transformation. This is the domain of the Holy Spirit, whose job is to restore our brokenness and keep us living in the costly freedom Christ won for us. If this phenomenon occurs physiologically, how much more so will God do this for us in our heart!

The Message paraphrases this hope we have beautifully: "I'll give you a new heart, put a new spirit in you. I'll remove the stone heart from your body and replace it with a heart that's God-willed, not self-willed. I'll put my Spirit in you and make it possible for you to do what I tell you and live by my commands" (Ezekiel 36:26).

The Thirsty Woman

There is probably no hungrier (or thirstier) person in the Bible than the Samaritan woman, whose testimony is recorded in John's Gospel. He introduces us to the Gentile woman who sneaks out to the communal well at noon to get a need met – the need to quench her thirst, of course. And in typical form, Jesus meets her in the place of her need. In fact, he prevents her from trying to meet it immediately, by sitting on the well and engaging her in conversation. Wisdom calls aloud in the streets and in this case He crystallises her painful history into one verse: "... for you have had five husbands, and you aren't even married to the man you're living with now ..." (Jn 4:18)

Having five husbands is a clear signal of a distorted appetite even in our modern Western culture, let alone the cultural setting of the Bible. She might think she's physically thirsty, but Jesus brilliantly uses her physical need to highlight her much deeper need of the soul. The woman has become entangled in a cycle of broken relationships, perhaps a result of her own infertility and an acute need to have her economic, social, and sexual needs met. Regardless of how she came to be in these relationships, we can be sure of the pain, rejection, and shame she experienced as a result. She has dined at Babel's Table to quench her thirst and returned even thirstier each and every time. Just as Adam and Eve did after they ate the forbidden fruit, she's hiding behind proverbial fig leaves. She's drawing water at noon, away from the watchful eyes of others who would have retrieved theirs in the cool of the morning. This is no surprise; isolation is the bedfellow of shame.

We don't know her upbringing, family of origin, or in fact any of the reasons her misdirected appetite led her to Babel's Table. The fact that none of it is mentioned communicates that none of it matters. Wisdom calls aloud to everyone, not special, clever people who have gotten it right for most of their life. Anyone who listens is welcome to dine at Wisdom's Table, and it's carved from the rugged wood of the Carpenter's Cross. You see, Jesus is not afraid of broken people. He doesn't recoil from our sin, sexual or otherwise. In fact, he leans in closer, and calls out all the more insistently: "Is anyone thirsty? Come and drink – even if you have no money!"

She drags her eyes upward from the man-made well in the ground and looks into the Well of Wisdom himself. He offers her one of the greatest earthly gifts we can receive: true and lasting satisfaction. John 4:14 "… those who drink the water I give will never be thirsty again. It becomes a fresh, bubbling spring within them, giving them eternal life."

A God Who Dines with Us

It is no accident that Jesus ate his way through the Gospels, nor that his parables were punctuated with feasts and banquets to describe his Kingdom. He did not just pray for prostitutes and tax collectors and lepers – he dined with them. Dinner parties in the Middle East carried a weight of intimacy and acceptance that is quite foreign to many of us in the West. But the message rang clear as a dinner bell in those small towns of Judea: Christ has the capacity to fill our souls until they are completely content and satisfied. The Samaritan woman ditched her seat at Babel's Table and dined instead with Jesus Christ.

He intersects us at our place of need, and then he meets that need the *right* way. Possibly the most redeeming part of her story is in verse 39, "Many of the Samaritans from that town believed in him because of the woman's testimony …" (NIV).

As soon as she receives Jesus, he commissions her to bring the Medicine to an entirely unreached people group. He saves her and sends her. This leaves us no room to assume that if you've got relational brokenness in your past that God cannot choose you, renew you and use you. All of us have fallen short, and usually those who have fallen the furthest fill their bellies at his banquet the fullest!

Revelation 22:17 "The Spirit and the bride say, "Come." Let anyone who hears this say, "Come." Let anyone who is thirsty come. Let anyone who desires drink freely from the water of life."

Breaking Up with Babel

The premise of this whole book has been about moving away from a Babel mentality and getting back to the Garden: the healthy, fruitful, wonderful environment God originally created for human relationships. We were evicted from the Garden in Genesis, and we've been trying to dig our way back ever since. We've learned that because it intimately engages every part of our being, sexual and relational sin carries a heavier price tag of shame, pain, regret, and brokenness. Rest assured that whether it is by our own poor choices or the fault of others, it never is, and never has been, God's will for us to live in these conditions. At the same moment the curse fell on relationships in the Garden, God made a promise: that the weight of that curse would one day fall on Another... His Son. Unfathomably, God extends more to us than forgiveness for our mistakes – He also offers to restore us to wholeness. We need not remain in the wounds of past hurts, sins, vices, and relationships that have left us with broken bricks and relational rubble. It is my hope and prayer that no one will close this book without being left with a distinct sense of hope and hunger for wholeness in Christ. Friend, if you're willing to pick up your ploughshare, it is yours for the taking.

Babel to Babylon

You may not realise that Israel's tabernacle (which later became their temple) was always meant to function as a makeshift "Garden of Eden." It was God's countermove to humanity's Tower of Babel.[1] His gracious answer to "let us make a name for ourselves by ascending the tower" was "let them make for me a sanctuary and I will descend to them"[2] (Ex 25:8). For this reason it was deliberately decorated inside with Edenic imagery to symbolise God's people moving back into the Garden, claiming back some of the evergreen territory the serpent had stolen.[3] Pomegranates, animals, and vine leaves laced the inside decor and cherubim (the guardians of Eden's gates from Gen 3:24) were sewn into the curtain veils.[4] As one entered the temple, it was as though they were re-experiencing the Garden not only because of the decor, but we know the manifest presence of God was located in the temple's holy of holies – reminding them that in the first Eden they had enjoyed unhindered access to Him (Gen 3:8). We might nickname this sanctuary "Eden 2.0"!

If you know Israel's narrative, you'll know that they got exiled from *this* garden as well. This is known as the "Babylonian Exile" and what an exit it was! It's significant for us that the word "Babylon" and "Babel" are identical in the Hebrew.[5] Evidently Babel sprouted from a tower to an entire empire called *Babylon*. (Think Babel-on.) This dizzyingly corrupt culture was luxurious, fast-paced, and seductive. Famed for their man-made bricks which reflected their extravagant and excessive culture, Babylon was an ancient version of Hollywood on steroids.

Israel became enamoured by the charms of Babylon and let it infect their heart and lifestyle. But Babylon doesn't play fair – Israel's captivation led to captivity: overtaken, deported, and enslaved. And don't you know Babylon was enriched by their slavery! After robbing their temple treasures, Babylon left it in ruins. The temple demolished, the walls crumbled, the gates burned. Make no mistake friends, Hollywood gets richer while we get poorer. The pockets of pornography moguls are currently being lined by the insatiable demand for sexually arousing footage. Casino owners gamble with people's livelihoods as happily as the soldiers cast lots for Christ's clothes at the foot of the cross. Babel gorges on our souls, leaving us skin and (broken) bones. We must understand that the temple and walls represented Israel's authority, identity, and reputation as God's peculiar people. Hollywood always looks fun and free until it has us in chains and our calling has burned to the ground. But Babylon was in the hearts of Israel long before they were dragged there against their will. Their inner brokenness was reflected in the wreckage of a temple that once resembled Eden. The reality of Babel is that it gets knocked down either way, and we're left living amidst the rubble and broken bricks of our own making. As mentioned earlier in the chapter on Boundaries, the story of Ezra and Nehemiah (which was originally one book, not two) record this huge undertaking of rebuilding the temple and its' walls. For them, rebuilding the temple and walls was in a sense like rebuilding the Garden of Eden, and with it, their destiny. If you too are living in the ruins of your own making, God will pick up your story here as well. God in His infinite grace has provided the scriptural pattern to rebuild *our* gardens! No matter how severely the enemy has ravaged it, God promises to restore us to wholeness. These are not whimsical words or wishful thinking – this is what the gospel offers us.

Breaking Up with Babel

So, let's begin the journey of restoration. If we slip into the sandals of an ancient Israelite for a moment, we'll see that their steps toward rebuilding began where everyone's does: repentance. What does repentance mean? In its most basic form, it means to "turn back, to return."[6] This is exactly what a Babylon-soaked Israel did. After years and years of living under Babylon's thumb, God's people were finally set free to depart and come home to reclaim their inheritance. Yet only a remnant repented and returned. Why? Because most of them became so enamoured by the luxurious and stimulating lifestyle of Babylon, they eventually assimilated to the point where they no longer even desired to change. Babylon seemed better than the hard work of repentance and restoration. They chose comfort over calling and missed out on the miraculous.

Romans 12:2 "... Don't become so well-adjusted to your culture that you fit into it without even thinking ..." (MSG).

It's a tragedy when God's people become so assimilated into the culture of our world that we no longer desire to be free from it. Everyone is offered the freedom to come back to the Garden, but not everyone wants it. The gospel promises us radical restoration no matter how broken we are, but the launchpad for transformation is repentance. We must genuinely desire to change and actively return home to the Garden Kingdom.

The word "repent" in the Greek *(metanoeō)* means *"to drastically change one's thinking."*[7] In our case, genuine repentance means radically abandoning the worldview of Babel and coming home to God's pattern of thinking. We need to confess our brokenness to God, acknowledging that the methods of the world are faulty, and God's Way is the only path to wholeness. There is no planting our feet in both camps here: we must decidedly depart from Hollywood and enter a new world through the Holy Wood of the cross. It's time to break up with Babel for good and pursue the path of purity.

Helper and Comforter

It is remarkable that Ezra and Nehemiah oversaw the ruins until *debris* became *Destiny*. Ezra was a theologian and mighty teacher of the Word who helped a repentant Israel return to the Scriptures. Nehemiah was a masterful leader who administrated the building process to completion. Psalm 147:3 describes the end result of applying the teaching of the Word and leadership of the Spirit to our aching hearts: "He heals the brokenhearted and bandages their wounds." The Word and the Spirit work together as Ezra and Nehemiah did, for the purpose of rebuilding our lives.

The name Ezra means "Helper"[8] and Nehemiah means "Comforter."[9] And guess what? Both names are precisely the titles Jesus gives to the Holy Spirit in John 14:25–26, best evidenced in the following translations:

NASB: "But the *Helper*, the Holy Spirit whom the Father will send in My name, He will teach you all things, and remind you of all that I said to you" (emphasis mine).

KJV: "These things have I spoken unto you, being yet present with you. But the *Comforter*, which is the Holy Ghost, whom the Father will send in my name, he shall teach you all things, and bring all things to your remembrance, whatsoever I have said unto you" (emphasis mine).

You see, restoration begins and ends with the Holy Spirit. He is the Master Rebuilder of the broken walls and relational rubble of our hearts. He is our Helper who bandages us firmly with His Word, and Comforter who leads the way to wholeness. He will rebuild our lives, conforming us to truth and transforming our appetites and behaviours. It is the ministry of the Holy Spirit that brings order out of disorder, just as the first mention of the Holy Spirit in the record of Genesis 1:2 tells us:

"Now the earth was formless and void, and darkness was over the surface of the deep. And the Spirit of God was hovering over the surface of the waters" (BSB).

The Holy Spirit took what was formless and desolate and brought order, design, fruitfulness, and life. He created a Garden out of the chaos and darkness. This is His ministry and my friend, His ministry has not changed since the first dawn. David's famous prayer of repentance in The Message paraphrase reads this way: "God, make a fresh start in me, shape a *Genesis* week from the *chaos* of my life. Don't throw me out with the trash, or fail to breathe holiness in me. Bring me back from gray exile, put a *fresh wind* in my sails!" (Ps 51:10–12 MSG; emphasis mine.)

If you study Nehemiah's strategy, you'd notice that he slips into Jerusalem unannounced in the dark of the night, to inspect the damage (Neh 2:11). No one dwelling in the rubble was aware of his arrival. While the broken-hearted were slumbering, he was studying. We may be in the dark night of the soul, wallowing in our wounds, but the Holy Spirit has already arrived in our life. He's looking over our areas of brokenness and vulnerability, ready to blow into the action of sanctification, upon our cooperation. Friend, wake up and open your sleepy eyes! If you have prayed David's prayer of repentance, rest assured that our Greater Nehemiah has already arrived into your chaotic and disordered brokenness, ready to bring order and life out of disorder and death!

Building What We Believe

While the Greek word for repentance centres on a radical change of the *mind*, the Hebrew term for repent is slightly different. It adds the weight of a radical change of *action*. For the Hebrew, true repentance is characterised by obedience. The Israelites who returned home from Babylon believed that their calling was to rebuild the temple and walls from the rubble of their past failures. But believing was not enough – they had to follow through with an action plan, clasping a tool in one hand and a sword in the other (Neh 4:17). They'd broken up with Babel, but now they had to do the hard work of transformation.

Paul the apostle gives us very powerful advice to help us overcome the negative effects of sexual, relational, and emotional brokenness. Romans 12:2 in the NIV tells us "Do not conform any longer to the pattern of this world, but be transformed by the renewing of your minds."

"Conform" means to comply to rules or standards. Words synonymous with conform are obey, follow, adhere to, submit to ... you get the idea. The Greek word for "conform" is *syschēmatizō* which means to be conformed to a pattern, somewhat like clay being fit into a mould with a pattern and thus shaped by it.[10] It is not surprising that the Bible likens us over and over to clay, since in a very real way that is how we began in the garden. God formed Adam from the soil of the earth. When earth is combined with water, what do you get? Clay. Clay can be moulded into all sorts of things, such as sculptures, pottery, toys, or writing tablets, if we're taking examples from Paul's day.

Romans 12:2 reminds us that the first human came from clay, and we remain no less mouldable. If we place ourselves in the mould of Babel, we will surely conform to its pattern of behaviour, values, and ways of thinking. Never forget that it is not just God who calls us to obedience and submission. Babel also seeks our obedience to its sexual and relational ethics, though it will use very different methods to enforce our compliance. Seduction, intimidation, accusation, and sheer threats barrage us at increasingly loud volumes. But if Genesis 2 tells us anything, it's that there is only one mould and one alone that will shape us into a whole human being with a living breathing soul: our Creator's Hands. Laying down our ego in submission to His craftsmanship is the only way we will be left with the finished product we desire: *Imago Dei*. To be whole and in this sense, *truly* human, is to bear the image of God.

Don't conform but *be transformed*, Paul unapologetically writes from the pen of a man who had experienced the transformative power of Christ in his own life. We are not transformed by an elaborate prayer, a fancy formula, or a magic incantation – but by the *renewing of our mind*. This is not a passive venture. Refusing to conform to this world's pattern requires us to actively conform to *God's* pattern of thinking. Babel philosophy is born of a corrupt culture and God has called us to not only uproot it, but actively build gardens in its place – and it starts in our mind.

2 Corinthians 10:3–6 tells us "The tools of our trade aren't for marketing or manipulation, but they are for demolishing that entire massively corrupt culture. We use our powerful God-tools for smashing warped philosophies, tearing down barriers erected against the truth of God, fitting every loose thought and emotion and impulse into the structure of life shaped by Christ. Our tools are ready at hand for clearing the ground of every obstruction and building lives of obedience into maturity" (MSG).

We must tear down our Babel-thinking and clear out the rubble of old thought patterns sculpted by a lust-driven culture. In order to experience relational restoration, we must change the way we *think* about sex, dating and relationships. Is sex merely for personal pleasure or is it an exclusive gift of intimacy for marital covenant? Is dating for selfish experimentation or is it a process of trust to discern who is appropriate to receive my gift of intimacy? Are relationships made to satisfy my own desires or are they a vehicle for the Kingdom of God, because I am made in the image of a relational Creator?

Changing our mind changes our thinking. Changing our thinking changes the neural pathways of our brain. Changing our brain changes our behaviour. And changing our behaviour changes our *life*.

This kind of change is what we call *transformation*. I apologise for the overload of Greek, but I've got another great one for you. The word for "transformation" is *metamorphoō* (μεταμορφόω) which is, if you hadn't guessed, where we derive the English word *metamorphosis*.[11] Metamorphosis carries much more weight than simply "a change". It's a transfiguration into an entirely different species; one which carries a new nature. Think of the caterpillar which undergoes *metamorphosis* when it transforms into a butterfly. It changes shape and form, becoming a new creature entering an entirely different environment with its newfound wings. It lives on a different diet because it has a new appetite. It lives in the air instead of on the ground. If God can do this with a caterpillar, of course He will do it with us!

Restoration is a Process

However, just like the butterfly who endures time in the cocoon, living according to our new nature is not an event, it's a process. The temple and walls of Jerusalem did not go up in a day. It required daily and relentless obedience from God's people as they stuck shoulder to shoulder in community, *building* what they *believed* in. If we think salvation is purely a spiritual experience void of engaging our emotional and physical state, we regard it like a button to press without requiring our own earnest involvement. However, getting saved does not mean God will wave His magic wand and all our wounds will instantly mend, our brain lobotomised, and our temptations vanish. We're immediately forgiven, yes. But rather than an overnight lifestyle change, more often than not people are radically and miraculously restored by a process. This process is called "sanctification", something Scripture tells us is the work of the Spirit: "God chose you as firstfruits to be saved through the *sanctifying work* of the *Spirit* and through belief in the *truth*" (2 Thess 2:13b, NIV; emphasis mine).

With this in mind, it's intriguing that the book of Nehemiah records no signs or miracles, in contrast to many of the other books in your Old Testament. The book of Exodus, where we get the pattern for *salvation* is dressed entirely in miracles, from the ten plagues to the splitting of the sea to the Mountain of Sinai smoking to breakfast falling from the sky. Yet the very book where we obtain the pattern for *restoration* (scholars nicknaming the Ezra-Nehemiah story the *Second Exodus*) there are no instantaneous miracles. Instead, there is an exquisite partnership of God's sovereignty and human responsibility. And you'll notice that God's people didn't build individually – and when it comes to restoration and healing, neither should we. Plant yourself in a loving and truthful church community and stand shoulder to shoulder with people who will champion your healing and pass you the tools on those days when you drop them.

Israel got their hands dirty as they cleared the rubble, laid the foundations, and raised the walls. This is not unlike the art of gardening. Gardening isn't exactly something you can do from a distance. It requires up close tending, dirt under the fingernails and sweat on the brow. God conscripts us into the rebuilding process personally, to ascribe *us* with dignity and *Himself* glory. It staggers me that Christ calls mere mortals to join Him in His holy work. He's not content to merely heal us, but obliterates our shame in the process by empowering us to join in with Him!

If Christ can renew our mind, this means he can renew our sexual metabolisms and sexual memories, bringing us to sexual wholeness and relational blessing. This doesn't mean He erases our memories, but rather renews the lens through which we see them. If you've made it to this chapter and you're asking: Can I, who has experienced relational sin and brokenness, have a meaningful and wonderful marriage, healthy sex life and bright future? Of course! But the restoration process varies from person to person, depending on their family of origin, personalities, and environment. For this reason, it's important not to look from left to right more often than we look up.

Not one inch of us is withheld from the transformative power of the gospel. Bit by bit, day by day, seed by seed, we grow an entirely new landscape in our mind that in turn produces the fruit of changed behaviour ... and eventually changed lives. If He waved a wand and our mind was magically altered in a moment, we may not have built enough fighting muscles, healthy habits, and strong thought patterns to resist the next time temptation and opposition come – and they will surely come.

One of the striking features of Nehemiah is that they built in the face of hostile and constant persecution which only increased as the project progressed. Nehemiah 4:1–5 records the scathing jeers and rage from two men who stood at the bottom of the wall as it was being built. These enemies, identified as Tobias and Sanballat, both had an inheritance of sexual immorality and incest.[12] We shouldn't be surprised when all manner of bullies come out of the woodwork and stand at the sidelines to intimidate us into quitting when we pursue restoration. Hollywood has an inheritance of sexual perversion, and guess what? Misery loves company.

Perhaps we tend to overlook the great miraculous power in a person transformed. A person becoming whole in Christ is not always instant; it may have even taken years – but when they stand before you like a trophy of restoration, it is truly a miracle to marvel. God sits outside the constraints of time, and the amount of it He chooses to take to bring us to wholeness does not diminish whether something is utterly divine. Nehemiah's wall was built in a gobsmacking fifty-two days! No, not an instant event, but the timing was nevertheless miraculous, and the glory was given to God.

Finish the Work

Let's not pretend that seventy years of slavery was undone in a short eight weeks. If you study the books of Ezra and Nehemiah carefully, you'll notice an unwelcome gap in the process of restoration. Tragically, those who'd originally returned had become distracted by building their own things instead of focusing on God's restoration project. Remember when God told humans to build a garden and they built Babel instead? Here we go again! For close to twenty years the foundations of that temple just sat there, and the people became used to operating on a messy construction site. Every day they walked among their half-finished restoration project, trying to function as best as possible in the conditions. They'd repented and returned home, and even begun to build their life again – but somewhere along the way they'd become distracted and deceived into prioritising other things – and this meant their walls and gates were still broken. Having no walls meant they lived in constant fear of enemy attack, since they didn't have adequate protection from intruders. To make matters worse, they became a target of mockery by the surrounding nations and lived in daily shame. A half-finished project is almost worse than if they hadn't started at all. At least they wouldn't have got their own hopes up or caught the eye of unbelievers casting a disparaging eye upon them.

Friend, please realise that the Enemy is content to let us live in this gap. We may be saved, having repented from our own Babylon and returned home to the Kingdom of God – yet many Christians live just like God's people many years after their return to Jerusalem. When the spiritual afterglow wears off, we can become distracted by our own projects or despondent because things have gotten hard – and so instead of continuing in our restoration journey with the Lord, we settle for living in dysfunction from past relationships and poor decisions. We live in fear, constantly on edge that the Enemy will attack us where he knows we're weak and easily tempted. We settle for a daily dose of shame, telling ourselves that we've been a poor witness to the unbelievers in our life, especially the ones who watched us turn to Jesus. At some point we passionately began the process of restoration, but our life now resembles an abandoned construction site, with scattered tools and unfinished walls. Perhaps you feel trapped by the way someone has hurt or used you. Or perhaps you feel that you've made your bed of sexual sin and now you must lie in it. Maybe cancel culture, religious legalism, toxic purity culture or some other warped worldly philosophy has convinced you that you deserve to stay where you are, and you're not worth the amount of time it's taking to be healthy and whole. The Enemy never ceases to use shame, regret, or anger to keep us where we are.

Friend, don't pause between the foundations and the walls. If you've momentarily abandoned your right to restoration, just like God's people did all those years ago, consider this your encouragement to pick the tools up again. Refuse to be robbed of the very *wholeness* we've been discussing in this entire book. If we abandon our restoration tools, we may never learn how to set healthy boundaries, protect our purity, or foster healthy relationships. Remember the two aspects of relationship that were cursed in Genesis 3 were vertical and horizontal (see chapter 1). Many gladly enjoy a restored relationship with Jesus but forget that He wants to restore our horizontal relationships too. It's a little like embarking on a project to restore our backyard garden; we might clear out a bit of weeds and even lay a bed of soil, but if we forget to continue the gardening process of planting seeds and watering them, we're stuck in the foundations and nothing fruitful comes of it. It is so important that we don't pause when we hit snags or difficulties but continue to rebuild so that when the season comes, our relationships produce wholesome fruit. Continue the work, ditch the distractions, and "… I am certain that God, who began the good work within you, will continue his work until it is finally finished on the day when Christ Jesus returns" (Phil 1:16).

Failure Becomes Fertiliser

This "sexually free" generation tells you that having boundaries will restrict you, virginity isn't valuable, and Hollywood humanism harbours *real* freedom. Yet behind the masks, makeup, and Instagram feeds, we see divorce statistics that yield pain through the generations. We see unfulfilled people trying to seek satisfaction in ways that do not satisfy. We see the perversion of something beautiful making men and women slaves to addiction. In effect, our generation has become a slave to its own sexual culture. And of course, bondage is Babylon's area of expertise. But our God doesn't want us to be in bondage to a culture that lands us in a cycle of brokenness and broken hearts. He wants us to be a son or daughter in His Kingdom, fully whole, and fully fruitful. Maybe you've entered into the cycle of relational brokenness that Babylon offers: The feelings-based, hormones-driven, sex-as-the-goal-orientated culture that flows straight out of Hollywood and into our screens, magazines, homes, and eventually our hearts – that is, if we don't guard them diligently. Maybe you're tired of leaving a string of broken hearts behind you. Maybe you're tired of *being* broken-hearted. Maybe you feel like you've missed the bullseye of God's calling because you've wasted your time, energy, affection, and emotions on fruitless relationships. Know that God is for you, not against you, and as the perfect Father, He wants the very best for you. He waits for you to forsake Hollywood and run to the Holy Wood. There is not one person reading this who is not stunningly empowered by the gospel of Jesus Christ to do so. There isn't a soul who is not worthy to experience the renewing and restoring power of the gospel. You've heard it right here: go there, friend. Wholeness awaits you.

Remember, this is a Garden Gospel. Every gardener knows that plants thrive when good fertiliser is dug into the soil. But great fertiliser doesn't come easy. It's smelly stuff composted from our leftover kitchen throwaways, but it packs the best nutrients for growth! The Cross of Christ turns the scraps of our rotten mistakes and odious offences into the richest compost in the garden. The grace of God can take our areas of greatest weakness and make them our greatest strength if we refuse to wallow in our wounds. Let's pursue not just *forgiveness* of our sinful habits but *freedom* from them. Friend, you don't have to escape from Babylon with nothing to show for it. Reclaim your evergreen territory and extend your garden. Make the richest relationships, grown from the most fertile ground. Who knows what beautiful things Christ can grow from the fertiliser of our failures? As for me, you're looking at it. You're holding pages full of fruit from the soil of my past shortfalls. I am no stranger to Babel, but many years ago after growing sin-sick, I broke up with it and followed my Helper back home. I have met my Ezra and Nehemiah in the person of Jesus Christ. God has used every bit of failure to fertilise the ground He graciously gave back to me. This is Grace. This is the gospel.

Endnotes

1. GARDENS AND TOWERS
1. The cause, set of causes, or manner of causation of a disease or condition.
2. Millard J. Erickson, *Christian Theology* (Grand Rapids, MI: Baker Books, 2007), 524.
3. Gilbert Bilezikian, *Beyond Sex Roles: What the Bible Says about a Woman's Place in Church and Family* (Grand Rapids, MI: Baker Academic, 2006), 19.
4. Craig G. Bartholomew and M. Goheen. *The Drama of Scripture: Finding Our Place in the Biblical Story.* Grand Rapids, MI: Baker Academic, (2004), 33.
5. Ibid, 34.
6. Theologian Carolyn Custis James treats this topic of male-female harmony exquisitely and comprehensively in her books *Half the Church* and *Maelstrom*.
7. Gilbert Bilezikian, *Community 101: Reclaiming the Local Church as Community of Oneness.* (Grand Rapids, MI: Zondervan Publishing House, 1997), 31.
8. Spiros Zodhiates, *The Complete Word Study Dictionary: New Testament* (Chattanooga, TN: AMG Publishers, 2000).

2. THE SEXUAL GOSPEL
1. N. T. Wright & Michael F. Bird, *The New Testament in its World: An Introduction to the History, Literature, and Theology of the First Christians* (London: SPCK Publishing, 2019) 158.

2 Ibid, 284.
3 C. S. Lewis, *The Screwtape Letters: Letters from a Senior to a Junior Devil* (London, England: William Collins, 2012), 44.
4 Beth Felker Jones, *Practicing Christian Doctrine: An Introduction to Thinking and Living Theologically* (Grand Rapids, MI: Baker Academic, 2014), 101.
5 Ibid, 102.
6 S. N. Williams, "Nietzsche, Friedrich (1844–1900)," ed. Martin Davie et al., *New Dictionary of Theology: Historical and Systematic* (London; Downers Grove, IL: Inter-Varsity Press; InterVarsity Press, 2016), 622.
7 J. Alan Branch, *Born This Way: Homosexuality, Science & the Scriptures* (Bellingham WA: Lexham Press, 2016), 6–7.
8 Ibid, 17–19.
9 Matthew S. Stanford, *The Biology of Sin: Grace, Hope and Healing for Those Who Feel Trapped* (Downer's Grove, IL: InterVarsity Press, 2010), 48.
10 Craig S. Keener, "Family and Household," *Dictionary of New Testament Background: A Compendium of Contemporary Biblical Scholarship* (Downers Grove, IL: InterVarsity Press, 2000), 359.

3. BIOLOGY THEOLOGY

1 Joe S. McIlhaney, Jr. & Freda McKissic Bush, *Hooked: New Science on How Casual Sex is Affecting Our Children* (Chicago, IL: Northfield publishing, 2019) 43.
2 Stanford, *The Biology of Sin*, 53.
3 Ibid.
4 McIlhaney & Bush, *Hooked*, 36.
5 Stanford, *The Biology of Sin*, 53.
6 McIlhaney & Bush, *Hooked*, 41.
7 W. D. Norman, "Endorphins," ed. David G. Benner and Peter C. Hill, *Baker Encyclopedia of Psychology & Counseling*, Baker Reference Library (Grand Rapids, MI: Baker Books, 1999), 401.
8 Patricia Weerakoon, *Teen Sex by the Book: A Call to Countercultural Living* (Sydney South, NSW: Anglican Youthworks, 2012), 169.
9 Luke 14:28.
10 Marg Mowczko, "Paul's Main Point in Ephesians 5:22–33", Marg Mowczko: Exploring the biblical theology of Christian egalitarianism, April 30, 2012, https://margmowczko.com/pauls-main-point-in-eph-5_22-33/
11 To simplify, Complementarians believe men and women have different but complementary roles in marriage and religious leadership, whereby the woman submits to the man's leadership. Egalitarians believe in equal authority and responsibility for male and female in the home and

ENDNOTES

in the church. Regardless of what stance we hold to, we can agree that Paul's emphasis is on the mystery of the Gospel being reflected in the covenant oneness within marriage between a man and a woman.

4. WHEN TWO BECOME ONE

1. I am indebted to Pastor Neville Strachan for inheriting years of his teaching on covenantal theology. Although I am referencing other esteemed academics in this chapter regarding covenant, it is Neville who has brilliantly pieced all this together for myself and many students over his decades of teaching ministry. When he writes his book on this subject, I highly recommend it!
2. James Swanson, Dictionary of Biblical Languages with Semantic Domains: Hebrew (Old Testament) (Oak Harbor: Logos Research Systems, Inc., 1997).
3. In several places in Scripture, covenant trumps the Mosaic Law (for example, Joshua 9 with the Gibeonites).
4. Scott Hahn, "Covenant," ed. John D. Barry et al., *The Lexham Bible Dictionary* (Bellingham, WA: Lexham Press, 2016).
5. There is debate over the precise number of *major* covenants that make up the structure of our Bible, and whether this includes the sub-covenants. 7 is the number of covenant (as well as perfection) and this is my position for various reasons. However, the number does not concern us in regard to the impact it has on modern marriage.
6. Scott Hahn, "Covenant," ed. John D. Barry et al., *The Lexham Bible Dictionary* (Bellingham, WA: Lexham Press, 2016).
7. Ibid.
8. James Swanson, Dictionary of Biblical Languages with Semantic Domains: Hebrew (Old Testament) (Oak Harbor: Logos Research Systems, Inc., 1997).
9. Ibid.
10. Douglas Mangum, "Blood," ed. John D. Barry et al., *The Lexham Bible Dictionary* (Bellingham, WA: Lexham Press, 2016).
11. George E. Mendenhall and Gary A. Herion, "Covenant," ed. David Noel Freedman, *The Anchor Yale Bible Dictionary* (New York: Doubleday, 1992), 1185.
12. Scott Hahn, "Covenant,".
13. Daniel Timmer, "Sabbath, Critical Issues," ed. John D. Barry et al., *The Lexham Bible Dictionary* (Bellingham, WA: Lexham Press, 2016).
14. Scott Hahn, "Covenant,".
15. Ibid.
16. Paul P. Enns, "Weddings," ed. Chad Brand et al., *Holman Illustrated Bible Dictionary* (Nashville, TN: Holman Bible Publishers, 2003), 1664.

17 Brides of Jewish antiquity wore garlands of flowers and a veil. We derive the tradition of white to symbolise purity from various scriptures such as Revelation 3:18, Isaiah 1:18, Psalm 51:7.
18 Anita Diamant, *The New Jewish Wedding* (New York, NY: Simon & Schuster, 1985), 68.

5. MEN AND WOMEN IN THE IMAGE OF GOD

1 Werner Gitt, "Dazzling design in miniature: DNA information storage" *Creation*, 6 December 1997, https://creation.com/dazzling-design-in-miniature-dna-information-storage-creation-magazine
2 Don Batten, "Cheating With Chance", Creation.com, 27 February 2013, https://creation.com/cheating-with-chance
3 James Swanson, *Dictionary of Biblical Languages with Semantic Domains : Hebrew (Old Testament)* (Oak Harbor: Logos Research Systems, Inc., 1997).
4 Jonathan Sarfati, "Eve, the rib, and modern genetics", *Creation*, April 2018, https://creation.com/eve-and-modern-genetics
5 James Swanson, *Dictionary of Biblical Languages with Semantic Domains: Hebrew (Old Testament)* (Oak Harbor: Logos Research Systems, Inc., 1997).
6 Spiros Zodhiates, *The Complete Word Study Dictionary: New Testament* (Chattanooga, TN: AMG Publishers, 2000).
7 Bilezikien, *Beyond Sex roles*, 22.
8 Stelman Smith and Judson Cornwall, *The Exhaustive Dictionary of Bible Names* (North Brunswick, NJ: Bridge-Logos, 1998), 241.
9 Mark Gungor, *Laugh Your Way to a Better Marriage: Unlocking the Secrets to Life, Love, and Marriage* (New York, NY: Atria Paperback, 2008), 160.

6. BOUNDARIES TO BLESSINGS

1 Henry Cloud & John Townsend, *Boundaries in Dating: How Healthy Choices Grow Healthy Relationships* (Grand Rapids, MI: Zondervan, 2000), 28.
2 "Walls" In *Dictionary of Biblical Imagery: An encyclopaedic exploration of the images, symbols, motifs, figures of speech and literary patterns of the Bible*. Edited by Leland Ryken, James C. Wilhoit, Tremper Longman III. (Downers Grove, England: InterVarsity Press, 1998), 92.
3 McIlhaney & Bush, *Hooked*, 39.
4 Andy Stanley, *The New Rules for Love, Sex & Dating*, (Grand Rapids:, MI: Zondervan, 2014), 27
5 Raymond Brown, *The Message of Deuteronomy: Not by Bread Alone*, ed. J. A. Motyer and Derek Tidball, The Bible Speaks Today (England: Inter-Varsity Press, 1993), 217.

6   Raymond Brown, *The Message of Nehemiah: God's Servant in a Time of Change*, ed. J. A. Motyer and Derek Tidball, The Bible Speaks Today (England: Inter-Varsity Press, 1998), 32.

7. DATING IN A DIGITAL WORLD
1   Bill Warren, "Shame and Honor," ed. Chad Brand et al., *Holman Illustrated Bible Dictionary* (Nashville, TN: Holman Bible Publishers, 2003), 1473.
2   Cloud & Townsend, *Boundaries in Dating*, 11.
3   Mark Gungor, *Laugh Your Way to a Better Marriage*, 11.
4   Choice, Stories Of" In *Dictionary of Biblical Imagery: An encyclopaedic exploration of the images, symbols, motifs, figures of speech and literary patterns of the Bible*. Edited by Leland Ryken, James C. Wilhoit, Tremper Longman III. (Downers Grove, England: InterVarsity Press, 1998), 144.
5   Inc Merriam-Webster, *Merriam-Webster's Collegiate Dictionary*. (Springfield, MA: Merriam-Webster, Inc., 2003).
6   Tom Gledhill, *The Message of the Song of Songs: The Lyrics of Love*, ed. J. A. Motyer, The Bible Speaks Today (England: Inter-Varsity Press, 1994), 19–20.
7   Caroline Leaf, *Think & Eat Yourself Smart: A Neuroscientific Approach to a Sharper Mind and Healthier Life* (Grand Rapids, MI: Bakerbooks) 2016, 24.

8. THE GIFT OF SINGLENESS
1   Alfred Plummer, "BRIDEGROOM'S FRIEND," ed. James Hastings et al., *A Dictionary of the Bible: Dealing with Its Language, Literature, and Contents Including the Biblical Theology* (New York; Edinburgh: Charles Scribner's Sons; T. & T. Clark, 1911–1912), 327.
2   Ibid, 327.

9. BABEL'S TABLE
1   David Atkinson, *The Message of Genesis 1–11: The Dawn of Creation*, ed. J. A. Motyer and Derek Tidball, The Bible Speaks Today (England: Inter-Varsity Press, 1990), 176.
2   Francesco Bianchi, "Desire," ed. Douglas Mangum et al., *Lexham Theological Wordbook*, Lexham Bible Reference Series (Bellingham, WA: Lexham Press, 2014).
3   David J. Sigrist, "Sin," ed. Douglas Mangum et al., *Lexham Theological Wordbook*, Lexham Bible Reference Series (Bellingham, WA: Lexham Press, 2014).
4   T. Longman III, "Woman Wisdom and Woman Folly," ed. Peter Enns, *Dictionary of the Old Testament: Wisdom, Poetry & Writings* (Downers

Grove, IL; Nottingham, England: IVP Academic; Inter-Varsity Press, 2008), 912.
5   James Swanson, *Dictionary of Biblical Languages with Semantic Domains : Hebrew (Old Testament)* (Oak Harbor: Logos Research Systems, Inc., 1997).
6   "Folly" Thesaurus.com, accessed Jan 18, 2021, https://www.thesaurus.com/browse/folly
7   T. Longman III, "Woman Wisdom and Woman Folly," ed. Peter Enns, *Dictionary of the Old Testament: Wisdom, Poetry & Writings* (Downers Grove, IL; Nottingham, England: IVP Academic; Inter-Varsity Press, 2008), 913.

10. BREAKING UP WITH BABEL

1   L. Michael Morales, *Who Shall Ascend the Mountain of the Lord?: A Biblical Theology of the Book of Leviticus*, ed. D. A. Carson, vol. 37, New Studies in Biblical Theology (England; Downers Grove, IL: Apollos; InterVarsity Press, 2015), 68.
2   Initially God's earthly dwelling place was the tabernacle, which was a large tent. The blueprint for this is given in book of Exodus. Later in their history during Solomon's reign, the temple was built using the same structure and imagery as the tabernacle. Both function for the purpose of housing the Presence of God and imaging Eden as that dwelling place.
3   See descriptions in Exodus 36 & 1 Kings 7.
4   Exodus 36:8.
5   Walter A. Elwell and Barry J. Beitzel, "Babel," *Baker Encyclopedia of the Bible* (Grand Rapids, MI: Baker Book House, 1988), 242.
6   Joseph P. Healey, "Repentance," ed. David Noel Freedman, *The Anchor Yale Bible Dictionary* (New York: Doubleday, 1992), 671.
7   Brendan Kennedy, "Repentance," ed. John D. Barry et al., *The Lexham Bible Dictionary* (Bellingham, WA: Lexham Press, 2016).
8   Stelman Smith and Judson Cornwall, *The Exhaustive Dictionary of Bible Names* (North Brunswick, NJ: Bridge-Logos, 1998), 74.
9   Ibid, 183.
10 Rick Brannan, ed., *Lexham Research Lexicon of the Greek New Testament*, Lexham Research Lexicons (Bellingham, WA: Lexham Press, 2020).
11 Rick Brannan, ed., *Lexham Research Lexicon of the Greek New Testament*, Lexham Research Lexicons (Bellingham, WA: Lexham Press, 2020).
12 Sanballat was a Moabite, whose ancestry and heritage comes from Genesis 19:31–37. They were the descendants and legacy of gross sexual misconduct through the incest of Lot's daughters. Tobias was an Ammonite, who were also the result of this incestuous perversion and as such Ammon was the cousin of Moab.

www.ingramcontent.com/pod-product-compliance
Lightning Source LLC
Chambersburg PA
CBHW020319010526
44107CB00054B/1908